HOW TO CHOOSE YOUR GCSEs

9th Edition

Alan Vincent

How to Choose Your GCSEs
Ninth edition

This ninth edition published in 2004 by Trotman and Company Ltd
2 The Green, Richmond, Surrey TW9 1PL

Editorial and Publishing Team
Author Alan Vincent
Editorial Mina Patria, Editorial Director; Rachel Lockhart,
Commissioning Editor; Anya Wilson, Editor; Bianca Knights, Assistant
Editor.
Production Ken Ruskin, Head of Pre-press and Production
Sales and Marketing Deborah Jones, Head of Sales and Marketing
Advertising Tom Lee, Commercial Director
Managing Director Toby Trotman

British Library Cataloguing in Publication Data
A catalogue record for this book is available from the British Library

ISBN 0 85660 968 4

Typeset by MacStyle Ltd, Scarborough, N. Yorkshire

Printed and bound in Great Britain by Creative Print & Design Group
(Wales) Ltd

Contents

About the author   iv

Abbreviations   v

1. Key Stage 4: an overview   1
2. Getting the facts straight   7
3. GCSE and the National Curriculum   11
4. How the GCSE exam works   21
5. Coursework in focus   25
6. The exam under examination   31
7. Choosing the right subjects   34
8. The vocational alternative   41
9. Before you make up your mind   47
10. Choosing the right GCSEs for your career   50
11. How has GCSE worked in practice?   92
12. The GCSE in Northern Ireland   100
13. ... And in Scotland   106
14. Life after GCSE: options at 16   114
15. Making the choice   119

About the author

Alan Vincent graduated with a French degree from Reading University. After teaching in Nigeria and Hertfordshire, he became Head of Guidance and Admissions for the North Oxfordshire Centre of Advanced Studies. Since 1994 he has worked as the Coordinator for the North Oxfordshire Learning Partnership. Until April 2004 he was also a SETPOINT, responsible for coordinating information based on Science, Technology, Engineering and Mathematics for the new Learning & Skills Council area of Oxfordshire, Buckinghamshire and Milton Keynes.

Alan is General Secretary of the National Association of Careers and Guidance Teachers (NACGT). Throughout his career he has made significant contributions to the development of careers education and guidance, for example through his involvement in training courses run by NACGT, ICG, CRAC, LEAs and other organisations.

Abbreviations

A-level	Advanced Level
ACCAC	Qualifications, Curriculum and Assessment Authority for Wales
ACE	Advisory Centre for Education
AQA	Assessment and Qualifications Alliance
AS level	Advanced Subsidiary Level
BA	Bachelor of Arts degree
BEd	Bachelor of Education degree
BTEC	Business and Technology Education Council (now part of Edexcel Foundation)
CACHE	Council for Awards in Children's Care and Education
CCEA	Council for the Curriculum, Examinations and Assessment (Northern Ireland)
CLCI	Careers Library Classification Index
COIC	Careers and Occupational Information Centre
CRAC	Careers Research and Advisory Centre
CRCI	Connexions Resource Centre Index
CSYS	Certificate of Sixth Year Studies (in Scotland)
D&T	Design & Technology
DfES	Department for Education and Skills
EAB	Examinations Appeals Board
ECCTIS	Educational Counselling and Credit Transfer Information Service
FE	Further Education
GCSE	General Certificate of Secondary Education
GNVQ	General National Vocational Qualification

GOML   Graded Objective in Modern Languages
H Grade   Higher Grade (Scotland)
HMI   Her Majesty's Inspectorate
HNC   Higher National Certificate
HND   Higher National Diploma
ICG   Institute of Career Guidance
ICT   Information & Communication Technology
IGCSE   International GCSE
KS   Key Stage
LEA   Local Education Authority
NACGT   National Association of Careers and Guidance Teachers
NNEB   National Nursery Examination Board
NVQ   National Vocational Qualification
OCR   Oxford, Cambridge and RSA Examinations
OFSTED   Office for Standards in Education
QCA   Qualifications and Curriculum Authority
RSA   Royal Society of Arts
S Grade   Standard Grade (Scotland)
SGA   Scottish Group Award
SQA   Scottish Qualifications Authority
SVQ   Scottish Vocational Qualification
UCAS   Universities and Colleges Admissions Service
VCE   Vocational Certificate of Education
WJEC   Welsh Joint Education Committee

1. Key Stage 4: an overview

Major changes are already in progress for the Key Stage 4 (KS4) curriculum, with others planned for the future. The Government wants to encourage greater freedom and flexibility for schools, so that they can provide a more appropriate curriculum – one that can meet the needs of all students. It is also keen for the curriculum to be sufficiently challenging for all students, whatever their ability.

What will this mean in practice?
The main changes to date are:
- Design & Technology and Modern Foreign Languages are no longer compulsory for all students.
- Schools have to provide the opportunity for students to take a course in each of four 'entitlement areas' – the Arts, Design & Technology, Modern Foreign Languages, and the Humanities. This is so that students can take these subjects if they wish to. At least one course offered in each entitlement area must lead to an approved qualification.
- Science becomes compulsory from 2006 (currently schools are allowed to 'disapply' students from the subject if they are doing extended work-related programmes).
- The statutory curriculum will now consist of: English, Mathematics, Science, ICT, PE, Citizenship, RE, Sex Education, Careers Education, and Work-Related Learning (Work-Related Education in Wales).

What if I want to do more than one course in one of these areas?

Most schools will be offering at least two courses in the Arts area (Art & Design, Music, Dance, Drama and Media Arts) and some students will certainly study more than one arts discipline, while others will study a combination of arts courses. The same will be true in Design & Technology (where courses include D & T Product Design, Engineering, Food Technology and Textiles Technology) and in Humanities (including Geography and History). In Modern Foreign Languages, some students will continue to study one or more of the languages they learned in Key Stage 3 (KS3); others will study a language learned in KS3 together with a new language; some might study only a language they have not learned before.

Clearly, it will not be possible for students to follow more than one course in each and every one of these areas of entitlement. Some hard choices will have to be made and you should take advice and guidance from teachers, careers staff and personal advisers, as well as looking carefully at course content – and weighing up your own inclinations.

Compulsory Science doesn't sound like 'greater flexibility' to me

No, but the Government takes the view that everyone needs a basic understanding of science and technology. It has acknowledged that a traditional approach to science does not suit all and has therefore introduced a new, shorter programme of study. This small core will lead to a range of new science qualifications, including a new single award GCSE. However, it is expected that most students will spend the same amount of time on Science as they do now, taking courses that lead to the equivalent of a double award GCSE.

What is special about this new approach to Science?

The new core single award for Science is intended to develop 'scientific literacy'. In this new century, relatively few will become professional scientists or technologists, but there is an increasing need for us all to have a high level of awareness and understanding about the way that science and technology help shape our lives. The Government's intention is to prepare students for their future roles as consumers and citizens. For example, the compulsory core will include issues like genetic engineering and space exploration.

The double award will continue, but will be adapted to allow alternative progression routes for those who wish to:

1. take 'general' modules and prepare for the more advanced study required for careers in engineering and medicine, or
2. take 'applied' modules and develop the practical scientific capability needed for jobs in e.g. health care, agriculture, manufacturing, communications and technical quality assurance.

What is an 'approved qualification'?

It is an external qualification that has been approved by the Secretary of State. There are approved qualifications for students at KS4 at a range of levels. All these qualifications are listed in Section 96 of the Learning and Skills Act 2000, published by the DfES. The list can be viewed at www.dfes.gov.uk/section96.

And you said that Work-Related Learning is also compulsory. What will that mean?

Yes, from September 2004 it will become a statutory requirement that all young people should experience some Work-Related Learning at KS4. The idea is that all young people need to learn *through* experience of work, to learn *about* work and working practices, and to learn the *skills for* work. All students should be able to benefit from such experience, which may e.g. include enterprise education, work-based experience, or links with careers education or citizenship.

There are two aspects to the requirement for Work-Related Learning. Firstly, schools must provide Work-Related Learning for all students. Then there is also a non-statutory framework that sets out the minimum that schools should be providing for all students. It should be entirely possible for schools to deliver the minimum requirement for Work-Related Learning across the curriculum – and not have to treat it as a separate subject with its own curriculum time.

Will there be examinations in Work-Related Learning?

If schools are interested in accrediting work-related learning, there are a number of qualifications on the QCA approved list. For example, OCR has a range of qualifications, covering both preparation for employment and career planning (including job-seeking skills). These qualifications go from Entry Level 3 (below G grade at GCSE) up to Level 2 (GCSE A*–C). The National Open College Network has a Certificate in Careers Education and Preparation for Working Life which counts for two GCSEs.

Where does work experience fit into this?
Preparation for Employment qualifications include work experience and are designed to help students develop their workplace skills, while also providing an extra qualification.

What if my school is not able or equipped to provide the sort of vocational or work-related courses that I would like to do?
Remember that Work-Related Learning must be delivered in all schools from September 2004. It will be difficult for most schools to provide a full range of vocational courses. However, many schools are now working with other partners, particularly further education colleges, to provide Increased Flexibility Programmes. These programmes allow some KS4 students to follow courses not provided at their own school. The courses lead to vocational qualifications, such as GCSEs in vocational subjects or NVQs.

Are there any other changes?
There are further major changes in the pipeline. The Government has set up an important working group to look at the overall reform of 14–19 education and training provision. The Tomlinson Working Group on 14–19 Reform is due to publish its final report in September 2004 and the Government will then decide how far to adopt its recommendations.

The Working Group made its Interim Report in February 2004, and the biggest change recommended is the introduction of a new diploma framework for 14–19, with less emphasis on a break at 16. This will mean that
- young people would work towards a diploma qualification covering the whole of their programme, rather than existing individual qualifications, such as GCSEs, GNVQs, A-levels and NVQs
- the award of the diplomas would be at the four levels of the National Qualifications Framework: Entry (equivalent to the present Entry Level Certificates), Foundation (GCSE at grades

A*–C, Intermediate GNVQ, and Level 2 NVQ), Intermediate (GCSE at grades D–G, Foundation GNVQ, and Level 1 NVQ) and Advanced (AS and A-level, Level 3 NVQ, and Advanced Extension Award)

- to achieve a diploma, young people would complete a mixture of specialist, general and supplementary learning, with learners able to choose from a variety of modular options within their overall diploma
- some existing GCSE, A-level, NVQ or other courses would probably become components within the new diploma
- there would be fewer written examinations than now, with more assessment by teachers, for example.

So, will GCSE continue?
There is now more emphasis on a 14–19 phase of education and the Government is encouraging young people to remain in structured learning or training until at least age 19. It therefore seems likely that GCSE will become even less of an end point at age 16. It will probably survive in some form, though, as an important and effective progress check for almost the full range of education and training routes. Young people will continue to need a way of assessing how they are shaping up for their preferred choice of further or higher education, training and employment. The Tomlinson Working Group Interim Report favours an evolutionary approach and is saying that the new diploma qualifications would grow out of existing programmes, such as GCSE, AS and A-level programmes.

What is this business about entry levels and other levels?
All qualifications approved by QCA on behalf of the Government are allocated to a certain level. This is so that they can be compared with each other and so that learners can progress from one level to the next.

GCSEs cover the Foundation and Intermediate levels (levels 1 and 2). Grades D–G are level 1 and grades A*–C are level 2. A-levels are level 3.

Where can I find out more about all these changes?
The QCA has a dedicated 14–19 learning website, at www.qca.org.uk/14-19. As well as giving support and guidance to

schools and colleges in managing the whole 14–19 phase of education, it aims to help students get the best from their experience of the phase. There are special sections of the website for students and their parents.

2. Getting the facts straight

The GCSE countdown for you has now begun. What are you letting yourself in for? Let's begin by getting a few of the facts straight.

What is the GCSE?
GCSE stands for the General Certificate of Secondary Education.

Who is the GCSE for?
YOU. It is designed as a two-year course of study for students in Years 10 and 11 (Years 11 and 12 in Northern Ireland).

At KS4, GCSE is the main means of assessing attainment. The criteria for GCSE examinations are in line with the National Curriculum for KS4.

Can everybody take the GCSE?
Yes. The GCSE is open to anyone who can meet its requirements, regardless of their age or circumstances of study. So the GCSE is available to both mature and private candidates, as well as to all those in schools and colleges.

In the year 2003, almost 6 million GCSE entries, or about 24 million papers, were marked by the awarding bodies.

When do I take the exam?
The usual age to sit the end-of-course exam is 16, but there are no hard and fast rules. You can take it before or after that age.

There is some more information about taking the GCSE early and its implications in the next chapter, 'GCSE and the National Curriculum'.

When can I sit the exam?
There are two sittings each year. Most students will take the exam in the summer, when all subjects are on offer. In most subjects, the exams are held in the period from mid-May to the end of June. The awarding bodies organise a common timetable, so that the different written examinations for the main subjects all take place at the same time.

Oral tests for Modern Foreign Languages and English speaking and listening tests are usually taken earlier, with dates set by schools, within a timescale laid down by the awarding bodies.

Some changes were introduced to the normal schedule from summer 2001. GCSE written papers in English Literature and Geography were moved back from May to June, in order to give teachers more time to prepare students. Some papers in subjects with fewer entries were brought forward from June to May.

The second sitting – most commonly used for 'resits' in subjects like English, Mathematics and Science – is usually in November.

So it's possible to re-take a GCSE exam?
Yes – and you can also carry forward moderated coursework marks from the first sitting to the next. This can only be done once and must be within a year from the first set of results.

What are the awarding bodies?
These are the organisations that design the syllabuses for GCSE examinations, within criteria set by the national qualifications authorities. For England and Wales, there are now only four awarding bodies.

AQA (Northern Office)
Devas Street
Manchester M15 6EX
Tel: 0161 953 1180
Website: www.aqa.org.uk

AQA (Southern Office)
Stag Hill House
Guildford
Surrey GU2 5XJ
Tel: 01483 506506
Website: www.aqa.org.uk

Edexcel Foundation
Stewart House
32 Russell Square
London WC1B 5DP
Tel: 020 7393 4444
Website: www.edexcel.org.uk

OCR
Syndicate Buildings
1 Hills Road
Cambridge CB1 2EU
Tel: 01223 553311
Website: www.ocr.org.uk

Welsh Joint Education Committee
245 Western Avenue
Cardiff CF5 2YX
Tel: 029 2026 5000
Website: www.wjec.co.uk

Most schools select more than one awarding body. Teachers can then choose the GCSE syllabus which they think best meets their students' needs. Remember, though, that all the syllabuses are based on the same National Curriculum programmes of study.

Why do I need to take the GCSE?

The age of 16 is a turning point in every young person's life. It's a time of change. Some of you may leave school and take a job or start on a training placement. Most of you will stay on in full-time education, at either school or college, for at least one or two more years, in order to improve your range of skills and qualifications. For some, the aim will be to take further examinations, like

AS/A-levels or a General National Vocational Qualification (GNVQ), and perhaps go on to university or a college of higher education.

For all young people, GCSE offers an opportunity to assess your skills and abilities and help you decide how you can improve these and use them to direct you along more specific lines.

What makes the GCSE different from examinations in the past?

GCSE is designed to relate to students' everyday lives. For example, syllabuses cover economic, political, social and environmental matters, where these are relevant to the particular subject. They also provide opportunities for the appropriate use of Information & Communication Technology (ICT), to complement and support work done in that particular subject.

With the GCSE, there is more emphasis on problem solving and using the knowledge you have gained. That is why GCSE courses include practical work, oral work, fieldwork, investigations, projects and even group work. As a result, courses are more interesting, more inventive and more useful. It all means less time being a passive learner and more time spent on projects, problem solving and finding out for yourself.

Most GCSEs include coursework – that's work that you do during the two years. And the marks for your coursework count towards your final result. Exams are fine for testing knowledge and, to some extent, understanding. But they favour people with a good memory and there are many skills which an exam can't test at all. How, for example, can an exam show how good you are at looking up information and using it? Or at carrying out your own project? The GCSE format will test not only your knowledge of formulae for scientific experiments, but also how well you apply them in the lab. After all, what use is it being able to remember something you don't understand and are not able to use?

This is where the GCSE scores – it is designed to test ALL your skills.

3. GCSE and the National Curriculum

What is the National Curriculum?
The Education Reform Act of 1988 requires all maintained schools to provide a broad and balanced curriculum for students of compulsory school age. This is known as the National Curriculum.

What subjects are included in the National Curriculum?
Basically, the National Curriculum consists of 12 subjects – with Welsh as an additional subject for Welsh-speaking schools.

In KS3, the following subjects are included in the National Curriculum:
- English
- Mathematics
- Science
- Design & Technology
- Information & Communication Technology (ICT)
- History
- Geography
- Modern Foreign Languages
- Art & Design
- Music
- Physical Education
- Citizenship.

At KS4, the range of subjects that students may study and in which they may be tested is increased, but the only subjects with compulsory programmes of study are:

- English
- Mathematics
- Science
- ICT
- Physical Education
- Citizenship.

In addition, all schools have to provide programmes for all students in Sex Education, Careers Education and (from 2004) Work-Related Learning.

From 2004, the study of Design & Technology and a Modern Foreign Language is no longer compulsory at KS4.

The only compulsory subjects in Wales are:

- English
- Mathematics
- Science
- Welsh
- Physical Education.

Wales also has separate Subject Orders from England in History, Geography, Art and Music, as well as in Welsh.

Schools in England and Wales also have to provide identified Religious Education, Careers Education and Sex Education. With Sex Education, as with Religious Education, parents can choose *not* to let their child study the subject (except for the elements of Sex Education required by the National Curriculum, i.e. human growth and reproduction).

How much PE and Games do I have to take?

The Government has stated its belief that schools should aim to give pupils at least two hours of physical activity a week, including the National Curriculum for Physical Education and extra-curricular activities. This applies throughout all Key Stages. At KS4, pupils can choose not to do competitive team and individual games, but the Government expects schools to continue to provide these options for pupils who wish to take them.

What effect does the National Curriculum have on GCSE?

There are National Curriculum guidelines on the knowledge, skills and understanding that all students are expected to have acquired in each subject by the end of each Key Stage.

GCSE is the main means of assessing what students have achieved in each subject during KS4. All syllabuses cover the KS4 programmes of study. These programmes of study define the essential content of each subject and are the basis for teaching, learning and assessment objectives.

There are also a number of approved syllabuses in subjects which do not have subject-specific criteria. These syllabuses are governed by the GCSE Regulations alone.

Will this make a difference to me? Will I have any choice about taking the National Curriculum subjects?

The National Curriculum takes some of the optional element out of the 14–16 stage.

Most students will take GCSEs in English, Mathematics and Science. For Science, you may take:

- a double award exam (equal to two GCSEs) that covers Biology, Chemistry and Physics;
- separate exams in these three science subjects; or
- a single award exam (equal to one GCSE) that covers all three science subjects, but less fully than the double award.

The Science option that you are offered may depend to some extent on your school's curriculum policies. Many schools encourage most students to take Double Science or the three separate sciences. The alternative Single Science course is intended only for a minority of students who need to spend more time on other subjects.

One important point is that the student who takes Single Science but who then wishes to take AS/A-level Science post-16 may need a bridging course before (or at the start of) the AS/A-levels.

However, there are important changes on the way for Science. A new programme of study at KS4 is being introduced from 2006. After that time, Science will be compulsory for all (see Chapter 1).

The National Curriculum is not intended to be a straitjacket and there is an increasing amount of flexibility. Already, in some circumstances, a school has been able to decide that a pupil will achieve better results at KS4 without having to take all the normally compulsory National Curriculum subjects. This is referred to as disapplication of the National Curriculum.

What does 'disapplication' mean?

It means that, under section 363 of the 1996 Education Act, a school is allowed to make exceptional provision to meet a wider range of pupils' needs.

At KS4, the school has been allowed to provide courses in Design & Technology, Modern Foreign Languages or Science which do not fully cover the programmes of study for those subjects. Over and above this, schools have been able to disapply a student from either *one* or *two* of the following subjects – Science, Design & Technology and a Modern Foreign Language.

However, from September 2004, neither Design & Technology nor a Modern Foreign Language will be compulsory for new Year 10 students. So 'disapplication' is no longer necessary in these two subjects.

While disapplication from Science can continue (until 2006), it can only happen in order to provide wider opportunities for work-related learning (you can read more about this in Chapter 8, 'The vocational alternative').

The regulations for temporary disapplication and disapplication for special educational needs remain unchanged.

Essentially, it is up to schools to suggest disapplication, but they should then consult with you and your parents (or carers). And you have the right to make the final decision – you can carry on with Science if you want to.

Formal disapplication may not be necessary for students to take on wider opportunities for work-related learning. Work-related learning becomes statutory in 2004. If what the school provides is still not considered sufficient for the individual student, there may be sufficient flexibility in the school's curriculum and timetable to allow you to take on extended work experience, for example – while still fulfilling the requirement to study Science.

In Wales, schools can use even more time as they choose, because the only compulsory subjects are English, Welsh, Mathematics, Science and Physical Education.

What about short courses as an alternative?

Short courses, as an alternative to a full GCSE, are available in:

- Art & Design
- Art & Design: Critical and Contextual Studies
- Art & Design: Fine Art
- Art & Design: Graphic Design
- Art & Design: Photography
- Art & Design: Textiles
- Art & Design: Three Dimensional Design
- Business Studies
- Citizenship Studies
- Design & Technology: Electronic and Communication Technology
- Design & Technology: Electronic Products
- Design & Technology: Food Technology
- Design & Technology: Graphic Products
- Design & Technology: Industrial Technology
- Design & Technology: Product Design
- Design & Technology: Resistant Materials Technology
- Design & Technology: Systems and Control Technology
- Design & Technology: Textiles Technology
- Electronics
- French
- Geography
- German
- History
- Information & Communication Technology
- Music
- Physical Education
- Physical Education: Dance
- Physical Education: Games
- Religious Studies
- Social Studies
- Spanish
- Welsh Second Language.

Some of these options are proving very popular. The courses are set at the same standard as the 'full' GCSEs but have half the value of a full GCSE. They take up half the teaching time – so they might, for example, be completed in one year rather than the usual two.

Short courses are graded on the same scale as the full GCSE, but cover fewer topics. There is no coursework for the short course GCSEs.

Short course exams often use the same questions and exam papers as full GCSEs. The same A*–G grades are used, and short courses are recorded as half a GCSE in the performance or 'league' tables.

You can use the short courses in different ways:

- more able students can use them as a way of taking more subjects, e.g. fitting in a second foreign language that might not otherwise be possible
- if other subject choices prevent you from taking a full GCSE, you can still gain a short course qualification in a subject
- if you think that you may need extra time to study a particular subject, taking a short course GCSE in the time taken by a full GCSE course may be an attractive idea.

Remember that you will be allowed to drop one or more subjects at the end of KS3, if this seems a good option for you.

Also, you will be able, either individually or on a whole class basis, to take GCSE early and then to drop the subjects that have been taken.

Finally, we include more information about alternatives to GCSE at the end of this chapter.

What will be the effects of my taking one or more GCSEs early?

There are specific National Curriculum Regulations which apply to whole classes of students taking GCSE (or equivalent) qualifications early. Students who take GCSE (or an equivalent qualification) in a National Curriculum subject at the same time as the majority of students in their class, and before the start of the second year of KS4, will from that time be exempt from the National Curriculum requirements relating to that subject. This exemption applies whatever the level attained by the student in the examination. However, it does *not* apply to a short course, when both a full course and a short course are specified for the particular National Curriculum subject.

The Government has encouraged schools to enter students for one or more subjects early if they are ready. It wants the number of bright students taking early GCSEs to increase, to encourage higher expectations. In practice, record numbers of students *are* taking GCSE early. Currently, about 45,000 take at least one GCSE before the age of 15. In 1996 only 30,600 took GCSEs before they were 15.

In 2000 two six-year-old children broke the existing record by passing GCSE ICT. In 2001, a five-year-old boy scored a D in the foundation stage of GCSE Maths – the highest grade available in that category. A special Government scheme was set up in 2001 to see 500 nine- and ten-year-olds sitting GCSE. The Secretary of State for Education thinks that eventually 5 per cent of candidates could be taking the exam by the age of 14.

The Government has recently raised the possibility of some of the most able students taking AS levels in some subjects at age 14 or 15. They would either be taking GCSEs early or skipping the GCSE stage altogether.

The Government is also investigating the possibility of reducing the time that young people spend in KS3. Some schools are already piloting this solution, which would allow students more time to prepare for their GCSEs or to take them early.

What are the alternatives to GCSE?

GNVQ has been a popular alternative, but is now being largely replaced by GCSEs in vocational subjects.

For more information about GCSEs in vocational subjects and GNVQs at KS4, see Chapter 8 – 'The vocational alternative'. Additional information about Vocational A-levels (VCEs) and GNVQs post-16 is contained in Chapter 14 – 'Life after GCSE'.

What about Key Skills?

All young people should be developing a range of 'key skills' that will be helpful to them in further education and training, at work and in life generally. The Government has recently confirmed that Key Skills should be seen as an essential component of the new, broader, more flexible curriculum. The National Curriculum is the main vehicle for the development of the Key Skills. Chapter 8 contains important information about Key Skills in the context of the vocational options.

Is there anything else?

Yes. More able 14- to 16-year-olds can by-pass some subjects at GCSE, by taking an Advanced Subsidiary (AS) course in Modern Languages and/or Design & Technology. Taking AS at 16 allows these gifted students to take A-level a year earlier, at age 17. It may also be possible for some young people to drop a particular subject in order to concentrate on other subjects.

While GNVQs and GCSEs in vocational subjects are about work, they do not offer training for a particular job. This is more the role of NVQs (National Vocational Qualifications). These are normally available for people who have left school and are already at work or in training placements. At KS4, some students may work towards an NVQ or NVQ units, if they are on a regular or 'extended' work experience placement, following a course at a further education college and/or working with a training provider. There is more information about NVQs in Chapter 8, 'The vocational alternative'.

What if I might find GCSEs too difficult?

There are increasing opportunities for students who are unlikely to achieve GCSE grade G, Foundation GNVQ or NVQ level 1. 'Entry Level' awards are available in a range of subjects and in vocational areas such as Hairdressing, Office Practice, Retail and Travel & Tourism. These non-GCSE awards have to be approved by the Qualifications and Curriculum Authority (QCA), or by ACCAC in Wales or the CCEA in Northern Ireland.

Changes in the KS4 curriculum now allow less able or underachieving students greater flexibility, e.g. to take vocational language courses as an alternative to GCSE, or a practical science course which is equivalent to four GCSEs.

There are a few other qualifications that your school might be offering at KS4, below the level of GCSE or GNVQ. Such qualifications have to feature on an approved list published by the DfES and QCA. They include:

- certain qualifications in Literacy, Numeracy and Information Technology which are intended to offer progression towards GCSE or the Key Skills units
- some qualifications in other National Curriculum subjects.

Some students will not be entered for GCSE in a National Curriculum subject nor for a designated qualification relating to that subject below GCSE. For such students, teacher assessment of performance at the end of KS4 will be recorded, normally via the Progress File.

To recap, the main courses at KS4 are as follows:

* full GCSEs
* GCSE short courses
* full GNVQs in approved subjects
* NVQs or NVQ units
* Entry Level Certificates.

Where Welsh is a core subject, students will take Welsh to GCSE. In schools where Welsh is a non-core foundation subject, students will study Welsh at KS4, but not necessarily to GCSE. A short course is available in Welsh as a second language. GNVQ Welsh Language units are also available for KS4 students studying Welsh as a second language. These units consist of coursework, with short tests.

There is also an International GCSE (IGCSE). This is mainly for overseas students, but is also increasingly being used by some independent schools.

Important addresses in England and Wales

Department for Education and Skills
Sanctuary Buildings
Great Smith Street
Westminster
London SW1P 3BT
Tel: 020 7925 5000
Website: www.dfes.gov.uk

The Qualifications and Curriculum Authority
83 Piccadilly
London W1J 8QA
Tel: 020 7509 5555
Website: www.qca.org.uk

National Assembly for Wales
Training and Education Department
Cathays Park
Cardiff CF1 3NQ
Tel: 029 2082 5111
Website: www.wales.gov.uk

ACCAC
Castle Buildings
Womanby Street
Cardiff CF10 1SX
Tel: 029 2037 5400
Website: www.accac.org.uk

Joint Council for General Qualifications
Stewart House
32 Russell Square
London WC1B 5DN
Tel: 020 7393 4750
Website: www.jcgq.org.uk

National Curriculum website
www.nc.uk.net

4. How the GCSE exam works

There are just five awarding bodies that set examinations for GCSE and GNVQs at KS4:
- Assessment and Qualifications Alliance (AQA)
- Edexcel Foundation
- OCR
- The Welsh Joint Education Committee (WJEC) [not GNVQs]
- The Northern Ireland Council for the Curriculum, Examinations and Assessment (CCEA).

Your school will normally be free to select courses of study set by any of the awarding bodies. Most teachers look carefully at the full range of syllabuses to find the course that seems the most interesting and useful – the one they hope you will enjoy and do best in.

With different groups setting the exams in the same subjects, do standards vary?
In the past, Government statements and reports from HMI have raised concern about the consistency of standards. In particular, the awarding bodies were asked to apply more objective criteria and to be more rigorous in their approaches and procedures.

GCSE general criteria from QCA provide overall guidance on subject titles, the nature of syllabuses, assessment procedures and the general conduct of examinations. These general criteria require each syllabus to promote a balance of knowledge, understanding and skills. They also demand that student achievement in each syllabus is assessed through a combination of coursework and terminal examination appropriate to the subject.

In England, Wales and Northern Ireland the awarding bodies together form the Joint Council for General Qualifications. The Joint Council is not itself an awarding body. Instead, it provides a forum for discussion and the exchange of information. It is responsible for coordinating the work of the individual bodies and helping to establish nationally consistent practices. The awarding bodies, for example, collaborated over the preparation of GCSE syllabuses for the National Curriculum core subjects of English, Mathematics and Science. Each group put forward proposals to the Joint Council. From these proposals a range of syllabuses was agreed by the Joint Council for General Qualifications. As a consequence, for each core subject there are now syllabuses catering for the full range of needs.

All this ensures that syllabuses have the highest possible degree of consistency. QCA works closely with the Joint Council and the individual awarding bodies to maintain GCSE standards and to continue to improve the effectiveness and fairness of the system.

The Joint Council also issues appropriate information on behalf of the awarding bodies and makes this information available on its website, www.jcgq.org.uk.

How is the GCSE graded?
The grading system is based on an A*–G scale. The top grade is a 'starred' A grade (A*).

Examiners decide the grade boundaries for the award of grades A, C and F. The remaining grades are then awarded on an arithmetical basis. For example, for a particular syllabus the grade A boundary might be set at 300 marks and the grade C boundary at 220 marks. The grade B boundary would then be set halfway, at 260 marks.

In Modern Foreign Languages, there is a separate awarding system. A range of points – usually 7 – is available for each of the four language skills. GCSE grades are awarded on the number of points achieved in the subject as a whole. So, for example, an A grade is awarded for candidates who achieve 24 or more of the 28 points usually available.

In order to help parents understand the level of attainment signified by the GCSE grade awarded, 'attainment descriptions' are offered that relate to grades A, C and F and below G.

How difficult is it to achieve the A*?

There is no limit on the number of starred A grades awarded in any one subject. Results depend on the quality of the candidate's work and on where the awarding body draws its other grade boundaries.

What happens if my GCSE performance does not earn a grade G or above?

If that does happen, the performance is reported on the results slip as U (for 'unclassified').

How will the marks for my GCSE be decided?

In most subjects, the marks are made up of two parts.

Firstly, coursework done in Years 10 and 11 (Years 11 and 12 in Northern Ireland) is assessed. Secondly, an examination is held at the end of the two years. This is explained more fully in the next chapter.

Will I lose marks for bad spelling?

The old regulations on Spelling, Punctuation and Grammar have been replaced by something called Quality of Written Communication.

QCA has marking criteria for use in GCSE terminal examinations. They apply to all subjects where candidates are required to write in sentences (in English or Welsh). They apply to all GCSE written papers *and* written coursework, but not to multiple choice or practical tests.

For each GCSE subject, 5–10 per cent of the marks for each written paper can be deducted for errors in spelling, punctuation and grammar.

The assessment criteria for English and Welsh make additional requirements for linguistic accuracy. Performance in spelling, punctuation and grammar are factors in determining the candidate's overall grade.

Does this mean that dictionaries cannot be used in examinations?

Dictionaries and spelling aids are not normally allowed, except for certain vocational examinations and for candidates who are permitted to use a bilingual dictionary (after the school has made a special representation and the awarding body has agreed).

Following the latest National Curriculum changes, the use of dictionaries in Modern Foreign Languages exams is now banned. Candidates are allowed to use dictionaries for internally assessed coursework, but not in externally assessed exams.

Are there any special arrangements for those with a disability?

Yes. The awarding bodies have special arrangements to ensure that those with a permanent or long-term disability or learning difficulties are not disadvantaged in assessment. Special arrangements can only be made following an application from the headteacher or principal and this must be accompanied by medical or other appropriate evidence (e.g. an educational psychologist's report).

One fairly common concession is to allow up to 25 per cent extra time for written examinations, allowing candidates who have particular difficulties with reading or writing more time to read the paper and to plan and correct their answers.

This has sometimes been a contentious area, with some inconsistency in awarding-body practice. It is well worthwhile for parents and/or guardians to thoroughly explore the situation with school staff at an early stage, if there is any possibility of such arrangements being applicable.

Further information is available in the ACE leaflet 'Children with special needs – sources of help'. This gives details of other organisations that provide support for young people with special needs and their parents or carers. You can call the ACE publications line (020 7354 8321) for the leaflet or their helpline (020 7354 8318) for other advice. There is also a website, www.ace-ed.org.uk.

Do employers understand what GCSEs are?

Every attempt has been made to let employers know about recent changes. But you might still find yourself faced with a bewildered employer or personnel officer. Don't worry ... help is available. On the back of the examination certificate you will receive, there is an explanation of how the exam works.

5. Coursework in focus

We've mentioned 'coursework' several times. Now it's time to look at it in more detail.

What is coursework?
Coursework is work that is integral to the course. This means that much of it is done in class and is closely supervised by teachers.

It can take various forms, such as assignments in English, History, Religious Studies; fieldwork in Geography; practical and project work in Art, Mathematics, Technology and Science; compositions in Music.

Throughout your two years of study for GCSEs, your teacher will set specific topics for you to do. These topics will be marked by your teacher, and those marks will go towards your final GCSE results.

Why is coursework necessary?
As mentioned previously, many skills can't be tested by the traditional written exam: practical and oral skills, for example. Coursework gives you the chance to demonstrate the many abilities you have and so makes the final mark you receive much fairer.

Teachers, with support from the awarding bodies, are responsible for ensuring that students take on suitable coursework. HMI and OFSTED reports on quality and standards in GCSE examinations have found that both teacher assessment and the guidance provided by the awarding bodies to support teacher assessment of coursework are generally of a high standard.

You should note that there are signs that coursework demands may be reduced in the future. Already some private schools are entering their students for a new version of the GCSE which does not contain any coursework. The international GCSE is being offered in ten subjects and is intended primarily for overseas students. State schools have to offer mainstream GCSEs and there is no immediate prospect of a cut in coursework for their students. However, the Tomlinson Report (see Chapter 1) may eventually lead to coursework becoming less important in any future 14–19 exam system.

Which skills and abilities are tested through coursework?
Your performance in coursework will show if you are able:
- to research, collect, compare and organise information
- to work in a group
- to make accurate records and use your powers of observation through laboratory and fieldwork
- to plan and organise a long piece of work
- to use apparatus and machinery
- to communicate – and that means to listen as well as to talk and discuss
- to investigate, plan and design.

These are exactly the work skills that employers value.

Coursework also encourages students to work independently and helps them prepare for higher level studies, such as AS/A-levels.

When will I do the coursework?
In some subjects you will start coursework during the first term of Year 10 (Year 11 in Northern Ireland), while with other subjects coursework may not start until Year 11 (Year 12 in Northern Ireland). It will all depend on the syllabus.

It is important to keep up with coursework. Always try to complete work by the given deadline date. Many young people end up with a lower grade than their ability suggests because of their failure to complete acceptable coursework.

Yes, but when will I actually do coursework? Will it cut into my spare time?
Some of the work will be done in class; some will be done as homework. Though your teachers may say it shouldn't take you any longer than your normal homework, it's only fair to say it probably will take more time if you want to do well.

Is there coursework in all subjects?

Most Modern Foreign Languages include an oral, but there isn't necessarily any other coursework.

What percentage of marks is given for coursework?

There must always be an externally set terminal examination. In the case of modular syllabuses, the terminal examination must account for at least 50 per cent of the marks.

The weighting for coursework in other syllabuses is set out below:

Art & Design	up to 60%
Business Studies	up to 25%
Classical Subjects	up to 20%
Design & Technology	at least 40% and up to 60%
Drama	up to 60%
Economics	up to 20%
English Language	up to 40%
English Literature	up to 30%
Geography	at least 20% and up to 25%
History	up to 25%
Home Economics	up to 50%
ICT	at least 40% and up to 60%
Mathematics	up to 20%
Modern Foreign Languages	up to 30%
Music	up to 60%
Physical Education	at least 60% and up to 70%
Religious Education	up to 20%
Science	at least 20% and up to 30%
Social Sciences	up to 20%
Welsh	at least 30% and up to 40%
Welsh Literature	up to 30%
Welsh Second Language	up to 40%

Do I have to worry about spelling in coursework?

When assessors are marking coursework, just as with exam papers, they will deduct marks for errors in the English – for poor spelling, punctuation or grammar. You could lose 5–10 per cent of your potential marks.

It sounds as though I am going to have to take a lot of exams
It depends on how you look at it.

Your ability will be tested throughout the two years. But your coursework performance will in some cases enable you to go into the examination well on your way to a good grade.

What if six different teachers give me coursework at the same time – I'll be a wreck!
Coursework overload is a possible risk with the GCSE. Your teachers will be anxious to avoid overloading you. Nobody can tackle a great number of assignments at the same time and do them all well – and your teachers do want you to do well.

In a well-run school, coursework overload should not happen. Before the two-year course begins, teachers usually get together and work out a timetable for setting coursework assignments. But even the best-run systems can break down. So ... if you are given too much coursework at any one time, don't keep your worries to yourself. Tell your teachers about the problem immediately.

No doubt you will find yourself working harder than before, but remember that your teachers are not trying to work you to a standstill. It is in their interests as well as yours that you should do well.

Coursework is to your advantage
GCSE has been widely praised for allowing candidates to demonstrate what they know, understand and can do.

Coursework allows a wider range of skills to be assessed than is possible in a written examination. Evidence suggests that coursework assessment increases candidates' motivation:
- If you are a good communicator, you'll have the chance to prove it.
- If you are a painstaking perfectionist, you'll have the time to perfect your work and so earn marks for it.
- If you are a thinker, you'll have time to think.
- If you are a problem solver, you'll get the time to find the solution.

But ... it's no good leaving everything to the last minute with GCSE. You won't get through by copying someone else's notes the day before the exam. You'll need to work throughout the two years to do well – and work hard. Sorry, but there's no escape.

What if I'm ill when an assessment is due?
You'll find that the deadlines set for coursework are quite flexible, so the odd week, even a month, of illness should not set you back too much.

But what if I'm away for a term or longer?
Most teachers and awarding bodies are very sympathetic if you are ill, and will try to find a way for you to complete the course.

There are no hard and fast rules; subjects vary, and so do individual cases. But if you have completed enough pieces of coursework over the two years, they can usually assess how well you are likely to do, and give you a fair mark. However, one thing is certain. Both your school and awarding body want you to take the exam and will do their best to help you. So, if you know you are going to miss school for some reason, tell your teachers as soon as possible, so that they can make alternative arrangements for you.

What happens if I change schools in the middle of my GCSE?

In most cases, it should not be too difficult for you to change from a course set by one awarding body to one set by another, because they will both be assessing the same skills.

In addition, you might be able to transfer any coursework you have already completed. But – and it is a very big but – it depends on what subjects you are taking. The Joint Council for the GCSE certainly recommends that assessment across syllabuses from more than one awarding body should be allowed.

For example, it is much easier to move from one syllabus to another in Maths or a Modern Foreign Language than it is, say, in History, where you could be studying a different historical period. And in English Literature the set books are unlikely to be the same, so again transfer tends to be more difficult.

If you are well advanced in your original studies when you make the move, then arrangements can be made for you to take the exam in your original course in your new school. Your teachers and the examiners will try to do their best for each student, so your case would be treated sympathetically.

My teacher doesn't like me. Will it affect my assessment marks?
No. Equally, you can't be upgraded by your teacher either. You can rest assured there will be neither discrimination nor favouritism in your GCSE assessment. No teacher would allow any personal

feelings to influence the results of a public examination. Besides which, there are so many checks and safeguards that it couldn't happen anyway. And research shows that coursework is no less reliable than written examinations.

What's to stop someone else doing my coursework for me?

The work which you submit for assessment must be your own. Teachers have to certify that coursework has been supervised properly, and they are usually very shrewd: they know what most of their students are capable of.

If you copy from someone else or allow another candidate to copy from you, or if you cheat in any other way, you may be disqualified from at least the subject concerned.

If you quote from any books or other materials, you should state which sources you have used. And, if you receive guidance from someone other than your teacher, you should tell your teacher, who will then record the nature of the assistance.

Some teachers expect more of their students than others and so mark stiffly – how can the courses be completely fair?

Teachers are provided with resource packs for use in preparing coursework, together with examples of candidates' work from previous examinations to demonstrate the standards required. There are also opportunities to talk with other teachers and moderators from the awarding bodies at meetings, in order to standardise work from the current examination.

What is a moderator?

The moderator is somebody outside your school who will look at the work of your class in relation to the coursework done by other schools. If the moderator thinks your teacher has marked too harshly or too leniently, compared with other teachers, then the marks will be adjusted to bring them into line. So the system is doubly fair because more than one person will be marking your work.

Will I know what marks I get for my coursework?

Your school might tell you how well you have done in individual pieces of work, but you are unlikely to be told your overall coursework mark – after all, the moderator system may see it changed.

6. The exam under examination

After you've put in all the hard work over two years, what about the last hurdle – the exam itself?

Probably the greatest difference between school examinations and the GCSE examinations is in the timetabling. In most schools, the end-of-year exams are concentrated into approximately two weeks, maybe less; because most schools do not offer very many subjects, the exams come thick and fast, often two or three in a day. It's very different with the GCSE. Exams are spread over a much longer period of time, so you should find that your exams are well spaced out, with free days in between. Great – more time for revision! But then you are likely to need more time as you'll be tested on two years' work. The timetable for exams is drawn up well in advance, so the term before the exams start you should find out when you will actually sit each paper.

When I come to take my exams, will subjects clash on the timetable?

Each year the awarding bodies get together and draw up a common timetable to avoid possible clashes of exams for students taking subjects from different bodies.

Will we really all do the same exam papers?

No. In most cases, students sit different papers, appropriate to their individual ability level. This process is known as 'tiering', and most large-entry GCSE subjects are examined through a foundation tier covering grades C–G and a higher, overlapping tier covering grades A*–D. In this higher tier, though, students entered for the higher grade are occasionally 'marked down' to an E grade.

For each tier of entry, the written question papers will:

- be at an appropriate level of difficulty for the range of grades available at that tier
- encourage the more able to respond at a greater depth
- provide opportunities for the less able to show what they know
- use appropriate language.

In Maths, there are *three* overlapping tiers, and separate content is specified in the syllabuses for each tier of entry. The highest tier includes material targeted at candidates expected to achieve grades A*–B, but grade C is still available for students who perform less well than expected. The intermediate tier includes more material targeted at candidates expected to achieve grades B and C, with grades D and E also available. The foundation tier covers grades D–G.

Art, History, Music, Physical Education and Religious Studies are not tiered. In these subjects, questions can be set that allow all students to respond effectively at their own level. Examination papers are therefore designed to cover the full grade range, without the need for tiering.

Are short courses tiered?

Yes. The tiering arrangements for GCSE short courses are the same as those for the full GCSEs in the same subject.

Remember that coursework is another way of enabling candidates to demonstrate different levels of ability. Coursework has the additional advantages of a less pressured environment and the availability of guidance from a teacher.

Do I have a say in which tier I am entered for?

It's your subject teacher who is responsible for deciding which tier of entry will give you the best opportunity to achieve your best possible grade. The decisions are usually made around January in the year of the exam. The teacher will certainly consider how well you have been doing in this subject, along with the result of any mock exam. If you are not happy with the decision about GCSE entry, your parents or guardians have the right to discuss the issue with the headteacher.

It all sounds a bit complicated to me!
If it sounds a complicated system, don't worry. Before you get anywhere near taking the exams, your teachers will tell you which kind of paper you will be taking in each subject. They will also probably show you examples of what the exam papers will look like and you'll have a chance to try them out. Don't worry, you will be in no doubt about what to do, and what's expected of you, when you take the exam.

I just can't do exams, I go to pieces. Is there any hope for me?
The good news is that the GCSE does help people like you. If you choose the subjects that best suit you, work consistently at your coursework and then revise thoroughly for the final examination, you should do well.

Will the GCSE give me a fair deal?
Most people think so, and here are the reasons why:
- it is fair because it tests all your skills
- the courses are interesting and relevant
- the exam gives you every chance of succeeding at your own level.

7. Choosing the right subjects

Subjects that can be taken at GCSE (as full courses) in England and Wales

Accounting

Arabic

Archaeology

Applied Art & Design

Art & Design

Art & Design: Critical and Contextual Studies

Art & Design: Fine Art

Art & Design: Graphic Design

Art & Design: Photography

Art & Design: Textiles

Art & Design: Three Dimensional Design

Astronomy

Bengali

Biblical Hebrew

Biology

Biology (Human)

Applied Business

Business & Communication Systems

Business Studies

Business Studies and Economics

Catering

Chemistry

Chinese
Classical Civilisation
Classical Greek
Design & Technology: Electronic and Communication Technology
Design & Technology: Electronic Products
Design & Technology: Food Technology
Design & Technology: Graphic Products
Design & Technology: Industrial Technology
Design & Technology: Product Design
Design & Technology: Resistant Materials Technology
Design & Technology: Systems and Control Technology
Design & Technology: Textiles Technology
Drama
Dutch
Economics
Electronics
Engineering
English
English Literature
Environmental Science
Expressive Arts
French
General Studies
Geography
German
Gujarati
Health & Social Care
History
Home Economics: Child Development
Home Economics: Food and Nutrition
Humanities
Human Physiology and Health
Applied Information & Communication Technology
Information & Communication Technology
Irish
Irish (Gaeilge)
Italian
Japanese
Latin

Law
Leisure & Tourism
Manufacturing
Mathematics
Media Studies
Modern Greek
Modern Hebrew
Music
Panjabi
Performance Arts: Dance
Persian
Physical Education
Physical Education: Dance
Physical Education: Games
Physics
Polish
Portuguese
Psychology
Religious Studies
Rural & Agricultural Science
Russian
Applied Science
Science: Double Award
Science: Single Award
Social Science
Sociology
Spanish
Statistics
Travel & Tourism
Turkish
Urdu
Welsh
Welsh Literature
Welsh Second Language

How to choose the right subjects

Because young people frequently change their career ideas at this
stage, most schools put some restrictions on your choice of subject.

The National Curriculum ensures that you keep your options open by avoiding narrow specialisation too early.

The National Curriculum limits the number of choices that have to be made by young people during Year 9 (Year 10 in Northern Ireland), but when there are still choices to be made, how should you set about choosing?

Ask yourself:

1. *What do I want to do when I leave school?*
    (a) If you know exactly what career you want to follow then turn to Chapter 10 and see what GCSE subjects are required.
    (b) If you are thinking of studying for a degree eventually, then take a look at a couple of publications that are likely to be available in your school or college careers library. *University and College Entrance: The Official Guide* and *UCAS / Universities Scotland Entrance Guide to Higher Education in Scotland* are the official guides published by the Universities and Colleges Admissions Service (UCAS). You should also look at *Degree Course Offers* by Brian Heap, published by Trotman. These excellent guides give all the essential information about the choice of higher education, including details of the subjects required for different higher education courses. In addition, ECCTIS (*www.ecctis.co.uk*) produces a computer database of full- and part-time further and higher education courses.
    (c) If you've no idea at this stage, don't worry – you're probably in the majority. At 13 or 14 it's rather early for most people to decide on a career. Your aim now should be to make a selection of subjects that will keep as many career doors open as possible.
2. *What am I good at? And what do I enjoy doing?*
    Are any of the available GCSE subjects closely related to these interests?

    Make sure you know as much as you can about the content of the GCSE courses that are options for you. Just to take one example, the criteria for History now require syllabuses to include 25 per cent British history. Also, some schools will soon be piloting a new 'hybrid' GCSE syllabus in History, which will link History to related vocational areas, such as the heritage industry, museums, galleries, historical sites, archaeology, tourism, media and law.

Now add any subjects you think are essential to your chosen career. Already you are beginning to get a list.

3. *Which subjects are most likely to be on offer at my school?*

Here is a list of the subjects most likely to be offered by schools.

MATHS

ENGLISH
Language
Literature

SCIENCES
Biology
Chemistry
Physics
Science – Single or Double
    Award

TECHNOLOGY
Business Studies
Design & Technology
ICT

HUMANITIES
Geography
History
Religious Education

EXPRESSIVE ARTS
Art
Dance
Drama
Music

MODERN LANGUAGES
French
German
Spanish

4. *What about other options?*

Before you make your final choice, remember – the GCSE offers a range of subjects you've probably never tried before. Many schools will organise a few sample lessons in the 'new' subjects they offer, to give you some idea of what they are like. These subjects could be useful, even decisive for your future career, so give them serious consideration.

You may still have a rather long list, so the next question must be:

5. *How many subjects should I take?*

As many as you are capable of doing well. It is better to get a C or D grade in six subjects, rather than a G in nine. It is well worth listening to the advice of your teachers about getting the balance right.

Coursework overload

Don't overburden yourself with coursework.

Some subjects involve more research-based coursework to be done outside the classroom. History and Geography are examples of this. Maths and Modern Foreign Languages, on the other hand, will probably include relatively little. As it is important to make sure you have sufficient time to do every project well, make sure you get the workload right by *not* picking too many subjects that are heavy on coursework. So, check coursework content with your teachers.

What are modular courses?

Modular schemes offer students the opportunity to study relatively small parts of the curriculum in a concentrated period. Each unit or module contains very specific and easily understood learning targets, with student learning assessed at the end of each module. The different structure of modular courses, with a heavy emphasis on assessment and systematic feedback between teacher and student, suits some students better than the more traditional structure.

In most subjects except Design & Technology, at least 60 per cent of the marks will still come from terminal examinations. In addition, end-of-unit tests which count towards the final assessment will be set and marked externally; and any marks allocated for coursework will be set at the same limit as for the ordinary GCSE in that subject.

And finally ...

Your teachers will see it as part of their responsibility to see that you are entered for the most appropriate subjects and syllabuses available. So, before opting for, or committing yourself to, any course, make sure that you ask each subject teacher:

- how much reading is involved
- how much writing is involved
- how much coursework is involved
- what percentage of the marks is given for coursework
- if there's the option of different tiers of assessment
- if there's an oral test

- if you'll have to gather information for yourself
- if projects are involved
- what practical skills are involved
- how much laboratory or fieldwork is involved.

With this information, you should be well placed to begin to make your GCSE decisions.

8. The vocational alternative

The Government is committed to expanding vocational learning in KS4. The main features include the introduction of GCSEs in vocational subjects and increased opportunities for pre-16 students to spend some of their time in further education colleges or in the workplace.

What are GCSEs in vocational subjects?
They are a new version of the GCSE, aimed particularly at meeting the needs of young people who want an introduction to a broad vocational area. They are practical in nature and give you the chance to learn by doing. GCSEs in vocational subjects can be mixed and matched with a range of other courses, including any other GCSE subjects, NVQs and other vocational qualifications, Key Skills, other non-GCSE ICT qualifications, and awards like ASDAN Youth Awards or Duke of Edinburgh Awards.

Are they worth as much as other GCSEs?
GCSEs in vocational subjects are double awards, so they are the direct equivalent of *two* GCSEs (like the double award Science GCSE). They are graded in the same way as other GCSEs (A*–G, with a U for Unclassified).

GCSEs in vocational subjects have been designed as two-year courses, although they are also available as a one-year programme.

How will I be assessed?
Of the three units taken within GCSEs in vocational subjects, one will be assessed through an examination, in either Year 10 or

Year 11. You can resit this examination, if necessary. The other two units are assessed through coursework. The coursework takes the form of your producing a portfolio – a collection of work that can include writing, videos, photos, tapes and evidence from adults (possibly your work experience employer, for example). Each unit carries equal weighting. The sum total of unit results gives the overall grade.

Double grades (e.g. A*A* or CC) are given, in order to reflect the double-sized nature of these new qualifications. These double grades are carried through as performance table points. Results are issued in August, in line with other GCSE results.

Are the awarding bodies the same as with other GCSEs?
Yes – AQA, CCEA, Edexcel Foundation, OCR and WJEC.

What subjects are available?
The subjects now available are:
- Applied Art & Design
- Applied Business
- Engineering
- Health and Social Care
- Applied ICT
- Leisure and Tourism
- Manufacturing.
- Applied Science.

How do these link up with the National Curriculum?
Some of these subjects relate closely to the National Curriculum at KS4. For example, ICT meets the National Curriculum programme of study for ICT (so you certainly won't need to take both a GCSE *and* a GCSE in Applied ICT). Both Manufacturing and Engineering will meet the National Curriculum programme of study for Design and Technology. And Applied Science can be used to meet the statutory requirements for Science, although it does not meet the full National Curriculum programme of study for the subject.

Where could GCSEs in vocational subjects take me?
They are mainly useful in giving you the opportunity to explore a vocational or occupational area that already interests you, perhaps

also to narrow down occupational choice within that broad area. For example, they are suitable for those who wish to progress to an Advanced Vocational Certificate of Education (AVCE) or other vocationally related qualifications.

Including GCSEs in vocational subjects in your studies may be of considerable benefit in enabling you to make a smooth progression into further education, training or employment. They can lead on to a wide range of courses, qualifications and jobs after Year 11.

Remember too that GCSEs in vocational subjects are not the only way in which the Government seeks to promote learning about work at KS4. While GCSEs in vocational subjects are available for all pupils, other types of work-related learning have been developed particularly to cater for young people who have made little progress in school work and who might benefit from more practically based opportunities. We talked about Work-Related Learning in Chapter 1. One of the reasons the Government is making Work-Related Learning a statutory part of the KS4 curriculum is the successful performance of young people involved in extended work-related learning. In the early programmes, about one-third of the students taking an extended work-related learning programme gained better GCSE grades than previously predicted. About half of these students improved their level of attendance compared with the previous year and about 60 per cent continued in full-time education or took up work with training after 16 – this was a higher rate than for other students with similar levels of achievement at GCSE.

What are the opportunities in FE colleges?

The Government's reforms of the education system include making it easier for young people to take up vocational options in further education – or with training providers (a range of organisations that organise training opportunities for young people). FE colleges – and some schools – offer other vocational qualifications in addition to GCSEs in vocational subjects. Examples are BTEC National qualifications, City & Guilds awards, CACHE Childcare qualifications and NVQs.

What is the GNVQ?

GNVQ stands for General National Vocational Qualification. GNVQ courses, like GCSEs in vocational subjects, are intended to provide you with the knowledge, skills and understanding you need for work in a broad vocational area. Students are expected to acquire the basic skills and knowledge relevant to the particular vocational area. Again like GCSEs in vocational subjects, GNVQs do not provide training for a specific job.

The courses are offered at Foundation, Intermediate and Advanced levels. The Advanced level was never available at KS4. The existing Foundation and Intermediate Part One GNVQs have been converted into the new three-unit GCSE in vocational subjects qualification. This brings it into line with the overall GCSE structure.

So GCSEs in vocational subjects are replacing GNVQs?

Eventually, along with other alternative qualifications. The GNVQs continue in the short term, but there is a schedule for the phasing out of the qualification at both Foundation and Intermediate level. For example, the GNVQs in Construction, Engineering and Performing Arts will have their last assessment in 2005. Other GNVQs will be taken for the last time in 2006, while the most popular courses, including ICT, Health & Social Care and Business, will finish in 2007.

In most subjects, students will be able to take either Edexcel BTEC qualifications or the GCSE alternative.

How are GNVQs assessed?

Awards are made at pass, merit and distinction grades. The weighting for assessment is usually two-thirds internal to one-third external.

Do I have to pass all units?

No. You can compensate for a weaker performance in some units with a stronger performance in others. The final grade is dependent on the total points score.

Can I be sure that GNVQs are as high a standard as GCSEs?

GNVQs meet strict standards approved by the QCA, the body responsible for monitoring the examination process and ensuring that awarding bodies meet the national requirements.

Can I be involved in NVQs at KS4?

NVQs are mainly intended for young people and adults doing particular jobs in specific areas. At KS4, some students may earn these qualifications through taking on a regular work placement, through a college course, or through working with a training provider. Students gain a certificate for each unit as they complete it. When students are ready, an assessor checks that they can demonstrate the knowledge, skills and understanding that they will need in the workplace, to do the tasks that are covered by the particular unit. At age 14–16, students will be working towards NVQs (or units of them) at level 1 or level 2. Level 1 is the equivalent to GCSE grades D–G, while Level 2 is the equivalent to GCSE grades A*–C.

Can you tell me a bit more about Key Skills?

There are six Key Skills – Communication, Application of Number, Information Technology, Working with Others, Improving Own Learning and Performance, and Problem Solving.

All GNVQ candidates have had to produce evidence of achievement in Key Skills in Communication, Application of Number and Information Technology. The intention is to encourage more integrated teaching of such skills across subject boundaries. For example, revision of the National Curriculum Subject Orders has taken account of GNVQ Key Skill requirements. So GCSE English contributes to Key Skill Communication, and GCSE Maths to Key Skill Application of Number. The National Curriculum programme of study for ICT (whether taken as a GCSE course or not) makes a similar contribution to the Key Skill Information Technology.

Candidates who have taken or are taking English, Gaelic, Welsh, Mathematics and ICT GCSE and GNVQ qualifications should be exempt from some aspects of Key Skills assessment when seeking that qualification. For example, a GCSE A*–C exam performance in ICT provides exemption from the external test in the IT Key Skill at Level 2.

The other Key Skills – Improving Own Learning and Performance, Working with Others and Problem Solving – are not formally accredited on the final award of a GNVQ. But GNVQ candidates have regular practice in them, just as they do with the mandatory Key Skill units. All Key Skills are acquired in a work-related context and this is one aspect of GNVQs that has made them attractive to employers.

But what happens to Key Skills if GNVQ is being phased out?
You should see Key Skills as an important part of your education throughout secondary education and beyond. A new Key Skills award was introduced in September 2000. Students at KS3 and 4 are able to achieve individual Key Skill units of the full Key Skills Qualification. GCSEs and GNVQs now have Key Skills 'signposted' within them. The signposts indicate where evidence towards Key Skill achievement occurs within work that the student produces for GCSE or GNVQ.

The Key Skills qualification will be available from GCSE to degree level – at National Curriculum levels 1–4. It is designed to be taken by all young people aged 16–19, whether they are in school, college, work-based training or employment.

Points for university entrance are also given for Key Skills, as they are for National Vocational Qualifications (the points system was previously based mainly on A-level achievement).

Each of the three main Key Skills is assessed through both a portfolio and an external test. Students who get at least a C in a GCSE in ICT will automatically get a new qualification – a level 2 Key Skills unit – worth 10 UCAS points, or one-twelfth of an A-level A grade. English and Maths GCSE candidates can also earn these points if they submit an extra portfolio.

Achievement at Level 3 in all three Key Skills will be worth 60 points, the same as a grade A at AS level. However, the Key Skills points are likely to be added up separately from the A-level points and then used as a secondary guide for university admissions tutors.

9. Before you make up your mind

Before you make your final selection, here are a few more questions that might occur to you.

Are all the GCSE subjects recognised by employers, professional bodies, universities and colleges of further education?

The honest answer is 'no'. If a minimum number of GCSEs is required by such students, these institutions (or individual admissions tutors or their departments) will sometimes not accept creative and expressive subjects like Art and Music.

The advice is: *CHECK YOUR OPTIONS ARE SUITABLE FOR YOUR LONG-TERM PLANS.*

But don't get the idea that subjects like Art and Music are not good courses to take. They are. It depends on what you want to do. For example, if you are thinking of becoming a graphic designer or an architect, then you should take Art. And that is quite apart from the value of such subjects in helping you develop a broader range of personal skills and interests.

Why do employers and colleges often ask for five subjects taken all at one time?

By asking for five subjects at one sitting, employers can expect you to be capable of coping with a lot of sustained work. It gives them a better idea of your all-round ability.

What are 'academic' subjects?

You'll hear people use the term 'academic subjects'. They are referring to subjects that are considered to involve theoretical work rather than practical skills. This distinction is no longer a helpful one, since it creates an artificial divide between the so-called 'academic' subjects and the practical and 'vocational' courses. GCSE has put increasing emphasis on relevance and practical skills, while most of the subjects labelled 'practical' or 'vocational' are intellectually demanding in at least some of their components.

What can I do if the GCSE subject I want to do is not offered at my school?

The best advice is to wait until you are 16, when you'll probably be able to find it at a college, where the range of subjects offered is sometimes wider. In fact, many sixth-form teachers and tutors suggest students take an additional GCSE as well as A-levels or other courses they may be taking. If, however, you want to take the subject before then, you may be able to find a specialist tutor, although this will not always be easy.

Can you get the top grade in all subjects?

Yes, but only if your syllabuses have been designed to include all the work necessary for the top grade or level to be awarded. If it is thought more appropriate to your needs, the syllabus in some subjects may be designed so that the work involved will earn, at the highest, a grade C. Similarly, it is possible for syllabuses to be designed so that the lowest level that can be awarded for the work involved is a grade E: see the paragraphs on tiering in Chapter 6.

Your teacher would tell you if a course you will be doing involves all the work required for the top level awards or if it is restricted in some way.

It is also important to remember that if you opt for an exam on high-level papers with, say, grade C as the lowest level available, you are *not* guaranteed that minimum. If you fail to achieve that minimum standard, you will be UNGRADED. In a typical year, approximately 5 per cent of candidates entered for the higher tier may not score sufficient marks to reach the minimum standard for grade D and are therefore unclassified.

**Why do I have to start selecting my GCSE subjects so early in
Year 9 (Year 10 in Northern Ireland)?**
A large school might well have over 200 students in one year,
choosing from quite a few different subjects. Drawing up a
timetable to suit everyone, including the students and the teachers,
is a major task. These days most schools make at least some use of
a computer, but it still takes time.

10. Choosing the right GCSEs for your career

This chapter will tell you the GCSEs you should consider studying if you have a certain career, or possibly several careers, in mind.

In 1999 a government-sponsored MORI opinion poll found that fewer than a third of GCSE students picked subjects because they liked them. Less than half allowed their academic strengths to influence their decisions. In by far the most cases subjects were chosen to help job prospects.

There are different ways of getting into many careers – but the usual method for most careers, and the *only* way for many, is through a RECOGNISED TRAINING COURSE or a DEGREE, PROFESSIONAL or OTHER COURSE.

There are other, less rigid forms of entry to some careers, and you will always hear about students who have succeeded in different walks of life without qualifications. But they are the exceptions. For the vast majority of us the only way is through qualifications.

To check the qualifications you will need, this is what you do:

- Look up all the careers that interest you.
- Write down all the GCSE subjects required.
- Make a list of all the different subjects mentioned.

This will give you a good base on which to build your choice of subject. You should do further research in your school careers or Connexions library and/or in your local careers centre library. The books and leaflets there will probably be filed under one of two systems. The newer system is the Connexions Resource Centre Index (CRCI), introduced in England only from 2004. The CRCI groups occupations into broad categories. There are 23 such occupational categories in the CRCI (listed here with CRCI reference letters):

A: Administration, Business and Office Work
B: Building and Construction
C: Catering and Hospitality
D: Computers and IT
E: Design, Arts and Crafts
F: Education and Training
G: Engineering
H: Environment, Animals and Plants
I: Financial Services
J: Healthcare
K: Languages, Information and Culture
L: Legal and Political Services
M: Leisure, Sport and Tourism
N: Manufacturing and Production
O: Marketing and Advertising
P: Media, Print and Publishing
Q: Performing Arts
R: Personal and Cleaning Support Services
S: Retail Sales and Customer Services
T: Science, Mathematics and Statistics
U: Security and Armed Forces
V: Social Work and Counselling Services
W: Transport and Logistics

Each category has an icon attached to it, for ease of reference.

In some schools and colleges, the occupational information is filed under the older Careers Library Classification Index (CLCI).

We have chosen to group occupations according to the CRCI, but also include the CLCI reference for each job in our listings. Whatever system is used in your school or college, your careers teacher, careers adviser or personal adviser will give you any help you need in finding your way around the library.

You can also use the Connexions-Direct website (www.connexions-direct.com) and Jobs4U (www.connexions-direct.com/jobs4U/) to research occupations in more detail.

Other booklets and leaflets that may help you to find out more about careers and courses at this stage include:

- *Careers 2005* (Trotman)
- *Occupations* (COIC).

And don't forget the range of computer programs that help you look at your interests and abilities. Some of them also produce a list of possible jobs linked to those interests and abilities. You may already have tried one of these programs but, if not, ask if they are available in your school or at the local careers office. They include:

- CID (Careers Information Database)
- Odyssey
- KUDOS.

The information given for each occupation in the following section is as follows:

Job title

Minimum entry level
Within the National Qualifications framework all qualifications fit in at one of six levels from the basic Entry Level (Level 0) to Level 5. Our tables indicate the minimum level at which you can reasonably expect to enter each particular career.

Essential GCSEs
This column indicates which subjects you should definitely be offering at GCSE (and remember that a higher grade (A*–C) will often be required).

Useful subjects
Those subjects where GCSE courses (or sometimes other qualifications, such as Part One GNVQ) are valuable.

Other academic/training requirements

CLCI reference
The final column gives the Careers Library Classification Index reference for each job in our listings.

In Scotland
As well as the different qualifications structure, there are also different career structures for some professions in Scotland. As a consequence, Scottish readers (or those anticipating a career in Scotland) are advised to seek more detailed information where it seems appropriate. One useful website for Scottish qualifications and careers is www.sqa.org.uk.

I'm Thinking About a Career in . . . Administration, Business and Office Work (A)

Job title	Minimum entry level	Essential GCSEs	Useful subjects	Other academic / training requirements	CLCI reference
Administrative/Business Management Trainee	3	English, Maths	Business, Geography, ICT, Language, Science	Variety of routes: eg business course after GCSEs or A-levels, direct entry after A-levels or degree	CAL/ CAP
Bilingual Secretary	3	English, Language (preferably 2)	Business, Geography, ICT, Maths	A-level in at least 1 modern language at higher levels; bilingual secretarial course after GCSEs, A-levels or degree	CAT
Civil Service Administrative Assistant/ Officer	2	English	Business, Geography, History, ICT, Maths	None before entry	CAB
Clerk/Clerical Assistant	1		English, ICT, Maths	Office NVQ training or direct entry	CAT
Company Secretary	3	English, Maths	Business, ICT	2 A-levels or BTEC National Diploma/ Certificate/SVQ2 or degree	CAP
Environmental Health Officer	3	English, Maths, Science	ICT	A-levels (including at least 1 Science), then degree or diploma in Environmental Health	COP

Entrepreneur	Entry/1	English, Maths			A
Executive Officer (Civil Service)	3	English, Maths	Business, Geography, History, ICT, Language	2 A-levels or degree	CAB
Health & Safety Inspector	4	English, Maths, Science	ICT	A-levels (often in Science), followed by a degree or HNC/HND in a scientific or technological subject	COT
Local Government Administrator	2	English, Maths	Business, ICT	Variety of routes: often at graduate level, but also after GCSEs or A-levels	CAG
Local Government Clerk	2	English, Maths	Business, ICT	None before entry	CAG
Personnel Officer	3	English, Maths	Business, ICT	2 A-levels and often a degree	CAS
Receptionist	1	English	ICT, Language, Maths	Office NVQ training or receptionist course is an advantage	CAT
Secretary/Personal Assistant	1	English	Business, ICT, Language, Maths	Secretarial course after GCSEs or A-levels	CAT
Specialist Secretary (eg Legal, Medical)	3	English, Maths	Business, ICT	Secretarial course (preferably a specialist course) after GCSEs or A-levels	CAL/ LAZ/ CAT
Tax Inspector	4	English, Maths	ICT	A-levels and degree	CAB

Job title	Minimum entry level	Essential GCSEs	Useful subjects	Other academic/training requirements	CLCI reference
Specialist Secretary (eg Legal, Medical)	3	English, Maths	Business, ICT	Secretarial course (preferably a specialist course) after GCSEs or A-levels	CAL/ LAZ/ CAT
Tax Inspector	4	English, Maths	ICT	A-levels and degree	CAB
Telephonist	1	English	ICT, Language	None before entry, but office NVQ training may be an advantage	CAT
Trading Standards Officer	3	English, Maths, Science	Business, D&T, ICT	A-levels (Science may be preferred) or equivalent; often graduate entry	COP
Typist/Word Processor Operator	1	English, Maths	ICT	Keyboard skills – through school or college course	CAT

Useful websites

Local government – www.lgcareers.com
Professional Secretarial Work – www.iqps.org
Scottish Local Authority Work – www.cosla.gov.uk

I'm Thinking About a Career in . . . Building and Construction (B)

Job title	Minimum entry level	Essential GCSEs	Useful subjects	Other academic/training requirements	CLCI reference
Architect	4	English, Maths or Science, Art & Design	Design & Technology, ICT	A-levels, Degree in Architecture	UB
Architectural/Surveying Technician	2/3/4	4–5 including Maths, English, Science	Design & Technology, ICT	A-levels or BTEC/SVQ award courses	UB UM
Bricklayer/Carpenter/Plasterer	1	Maths, Science, Design & Technology	Practical/craft subjects	Modern Apprenticeship/NVQ training	UF
Builder's Labourer	Entry/1		Practical/craft subjects		UF
Building Surveyor/Building Control Officer	Entry/1	Maths, English	Design & Technology	GCSEs or BTEC/SVQ	UM/UD
Building Technician	2/3	English, Maths, Sciences	Design & Technology, practical subjects	BTEC National Diploma/SVQ2	UD
Building Technologist/Site Manager	4	4–5 including English, Maths and Science	Design and Technology		
Cartographer	4	2–3 to include subjects from English, Maths, Geography, Art, Design & Technology, Science, Languages	ICT	A-levels or BTEC National Diploma/SVQ2	UT
Cartographic Draughtsman/Woman	2/3/4	2–3 to include subjects from English, Maths, Geography, Art, Design & Technology, Science, Languages	ICT	A-levels or BTEC National Diploma/SVQ2	UT

Job title	Minimum entry level	Essential GCSEs	Useful subjects	Other academic/training requirements	CLCI reference
Electrician	2/3	English, Maths, Science	Design & Technology, practical/craft subjects	Modern Apprenticeship/ NVQ training	RAK UF
Glazier/Roofer/Tiler/ Scaffolder	Entry/1		Maths, Science, craft/ practical subjects	Modern Apprenticeship/ Training	UF
Painter & Decorator	Entry/1	Maths	Practical/craft/art subjects	Modern Apprenticeship/ NVQ training	UF
Plumber	1	Maths, Science, Design & Technology	Practical/craft subjects	Modern Apprenticeship/ NVQ training	UF
Surveyor	2/3/4	5 including English and Science	Geography, Geology, Design & Technology	A-levels, Higher National Diploma, Degree	UM
Town Planner	4	English, Maths and one of History, Geography, Modern Foreign Language	Science, Statistics, Social Sciences	A-levels or equivalent, then a degree	US
Town Planning Technician	2	4 including English, Maths	Geography, History, Design & Technology, Economics, Science	BTEC/SVQ award	US

Useful websites

Architect – www.architecture.com
Architectural Technologist – www.biat.org.uk
Civil Engineering – www.ice.org.uk
Construction Industry – www.citb.org.uk
Engineering Construction – www.ecitb.org.uk
Surveyor – www.rics.org.uk/careers

I'm Thinking About a Career in . . . Catering and Hospitality (C)

Job title	Minimum entry level	Essential GCSEs	Useful subjects	Other academic / training requirements	CLCI reference
Chef/Cook	Entry/1/2		Home Economics/Food Studies, Science, French	Modern Apprenticeship or NVQ training, College course	IC
Domestic Staff	Entry/1		Home Economics/Food Studies		IC
Fast Food Shop Manager	2/3/4	4 including English, Maths	Home Economics/Food Studies, Business Studies	Business Studies or Catering course after A-levels	IC
Hotel/Catering Manager	3/4	3–4 including English, Maths, Science	Maths, Home Economics/Food Studies, Business Studies, French	Hotel & Catering Management Diploma/Higher Diploma, Degree	IB
Hotel/Housekeeper	1/2/3	4 including English, Maths, Science	Maths, Home Economics/Food Studies, Science, Art & Design, Business Studies	Full-time course	IC
Hotel Receptionist	2/3	English, Maths	Modern Foreign Languages, Business Studies, ICT	Modern Apprenticeship or NVQ training	IC
Kitchen Assistant	Entry/1		Home Economics/Food Studies		IC
Waiter/Waitress	Entry/1		Home Economics/Food Studies		IC

Useful websites

Careers in Food and Drink – www.springboarduk.org.uk
Hotel and Catering industry – hcima.org.uk
Pub and Bar Industry – www.barzone.co.uk

I'm Thinking About a Career in . . . Computers and IT (D)

Job title	Minimum entry level	Essential GCSEs	Useful subjects	Other academic/training requirements	CLCI reference
Computer Programmer	2/3/4	5 including English, Maths, Science subjects	ICT, Electronics/Design & Technology	A-level, Diploma, Degree	CAV
Computer Service Technician	2/3/4	4–5 including English, Maths	ICT	BTEC awards at National or Higher National level/SVQ2 or 3 in Computer Studies, Degree	CAV
Database Operations Manager	2/3/4		English, Maths	BTEC National, NVQ or Degree	CAV
Internet/Web Professional	2/3/4	4–5 including English, Maths	Science, ICT	A-levels or BTEC National, Degree or HND/HNC	CAV
Microelectronics Engineer	4	English, Maths, Science	Design & Technology/Engineering, Electronics	A-levels (Maths, Physics, Computer Science), Degree in Electronic Engineering	RAL
Software Developer	4	4–5 including English, ICT Maths	ICT	A-levels or BTEC National, Degree or HND/HNC	CAV
Systems Analyst	4	English, Maths	Business Studies, ICT	A-levels, Degree or BTEC Higher National Award/SVQ3	CAV
Systems Programmer/Software Engineer	3/4	English, Maths, Science	Design & Technology/Engineering subjects, Electronics	A-levels (Maths, Science), Degree in Maths, Computer Science, Electronic Engineering, BTEC/SVQ Awards	CAV

Useful websites

Computer Work – www1.bcs.org.uk/
E-skills – www.e-skills.com/

I'm Thinking About a Career in . . . Design, Arts and Crafts (E)

Job title	Minimum entry level	Essential GCSEs	Useful subjects	Other academic/training requirements	CLCI reference
Art Teacher	4	5 including English, Maths and Art	Design & Technology	A-levels, Foundation Art course, BEd or art degree, postgraduate teacher training	FAB
Artist	3/4	3–5 for formal training	Art, any Craft subject	Art training after GCSE or A-levels	E
Designer (Graphic, Fashion, Furniture, Interior etc.)	3/4	3–5	Art & Design, English, subject appropriate to specialism e.g.crafts, textiles/dress etc. Art portfolio.	BTEC Diploma or Degree in Art & Design after Foundation Course and/or A-levels	ED EJ SAJ ET
Display Dresser	Entry/1/2	No set requirements, but good GCSEs helpful	Art, practical/craft subjects	Art or design course	ET
Florist	1/2	3 including English, Maths and Science	Science, Art & Design, practical subjects	Usually Modern Apprenticeship/ NVQ training	OFM
Graphic Designer/ Illustrator	3/4	4–5 including English and Science	Design & Technology, Art	Specialist training after GCSEs or Foundation Course and/or A-levels	ED

Job title	Minimum entry level	Essential GCSEs	Useful subjects	Other academic/training requirements	CLCI reference
Museum/Art Gallery Curator	4	English, Art and Modern Foreign Language	Classical and/or Modern Languages, History, Design & Technology, Textiles, Science for specialist collections	Degree in Fine Art or Art History. Postgraduate or research experience	FAE FAE
Photographer	1/2/3/4	4	English, Science or Maths, Art, Photography	NVQ training available after GCSEs or A-level	EV
Press Photographer	2/4	5 including English	Art, Photography, Sciences		FAC

Useful websites:

Art and Design – design-council.org.uk
Crafts – www.craftscouncil.org.uk
Museum/Art Gallery Curator – www.chnto.co.uk/training/index.html
Art and Design Education – www.nsead.org
Arts and Creative Industries – www.NetGain.org.uk
Arts – www.artscouncil.org.uk
Photography – www.the-aop.org/

I'm Thinking About a Career in . . . Education and Training (F)

Job title	Minimum entry level	Essential GCSEs	Useful subjects	Other academic / training requirements	CLCI reference
Careers/ Personal Adviser	4	5 including English	Social Sciences	A-levels, Degree, Diploma	KED
Educational Psychologist	4	Maths, English	Science, Social Sciences, Statistics	A-levels, Psychology Degree, Teaching requirements	KEL
Nursery Nurse	3	2–3 including English	Home Economics, Music, Crafts, Science, Social Sciences	NNEB course, A-levels	KEB
Teacher	4	3 including English, Maths		A-levels, Degree, Teacher Training/BEd Degree	FAB
Teaching Assistant	1/2/3/4		English	Sometimes Nursery Nursing qualification or Modern Apprenticeship	FAB

Useful websites

Educational Psychologist – www.bps.org.uk
Nursery Nurse – www.input.demon.co.uk/careers-childcarenurserynurse.html
Social Work – www.socialworkcareers.co.uk
Teaching and Teaching Assistant – www.canteach.gov.uk/

I'm Thinking About a Career in . . . Engineering (G)

Job title	Minimum entry level	Essential GCSEs	Useful subjects	Other academic/training requirements	CLCI reference
Chartered Engineer	4	5 including Maths, Science, English	Design & Technology, technical/practical subjects, Modern Foreign Languages	Maths/Science (especially Physics) A-levels (or BTEC/SVQ equivalent), Degree in Engineering	RAB
Electrician	2		Maths, Science, Design & Technology, practical/technical subjects	Modern Apprenticeship or NVQ training	RAK/UF
Engineering Craftsman/woman	2	Maths, Science, English	Design & Technology, practical/technical subjects	Modern Apprenticeship or NVQ training	RAB
Engineering Operative	Entry/1	English, Maths, practical and technical subjects	Science		RAB
Engineering Technician	2/3	3–4 from Maths, English, Science, Design & Technology	Practical subjects	Technician Modern Apprenticeship, BTEC National Diploma/SVQ2	RAB

Incorporated Engineer	4	5 including English, Maths, Science	Design & Technology technical/practical subjects, ICT, Modern Foreign Languages	Maths, Science (especially Physics) A-levels (or BTEC/SVQ equivalent), plus BTEC Higher National Diploma/SVQ3/part-time Higher National Certificate, Degree in Engineering	RAB
Motor Mechanic	Entry/1	English, Maths, Science		Modern Apprenticeship or NVQ training	RAE
Sheet Metal Worker/Plater	Entry/1	English, Maths, Science	Technical/practical subjects		RON

Useful websites

Chemical Engineer – www.icheme.org
Engineering – www.enginuity.org.uk/enginuity/frame.htm
Science, Engineering and Manufacturing Technologies – www.semta.org.uk

I'm Thinking About a Career in . . . Environment, Animals and Plants (H)

Job title	Minimum entry level	Essential GCSEs	Useful subjects	Other academic/training requirements	CLCI reference
Blacksmith	Entry/1		Maths, Design & Technology, Engineering, Science, practical subjects	None before entry	SAW
Countryside Ranger/Warden	Entry/1/2/3/4		Geography, Science		WAR
Environmental Scientist/ Ecologist	4	English, Maths, Science	Geography, Geology	Science/Maths A-levels, Degree	QOL
Farm Manager	3/4	4 including English, Maths, Science	Business Studies	Diploma, A-levels, Degree	WAB
Farm Worker	Entry/1		English, Maths, Science, practical subjects		WAB
Fish Farmer	2/3/4	4 including Double Science		Diploma, Science A-levels, Degree	WAH
Fisherman	Entry/1	No special requirements	Geography, Nautical Studies	None before entry	WAH
Forest Officer	3/4	4 including English, Maths, Science	Environmental Science, Geography	Diploma, Forestry Degree (after Science A-levels)	WAF
Forest Worker	Entry/1		Science, practical subjects		WAF

Job	Entry level	GCSEs	Useful subjects	Further qualifications	Code
Gamekeeper	Entry/1		Sciences (for Biology, Rural Science and Environmental Science content), practical subjects		WAM
Gardener	Entry/1		Sciences (for Biology, Rural Science and Environmental Science content)		WAD
Groom/Stablehand	Entry/1/2	If you have some GCSEs, you may take equestrian exams	Science/Biology	None before entry	WAM
Horse Riding Instructor	Entry/1/2	4 including English	Science/Biology	None before entry	WAM
Horticultural Manager	3/4	4 including English, Maths, Science	Business Studies, Geography	National Diploma, Higher National Diploma, Degree	WAD WAB
Horticultural Worker	Entry/1/2		Science subjects		WAD
Kennel Worker	Entry/1	An advantage	Science/Biology	None before entry	WAM
Landscape Architect	4	5 including English, Maths/Science, History/ Geography/ Modern Foreign Language	Art, Biology, Botany, Design & Technology, Environmental Science, Geology	Diploma/Degree in Landscape Architecture	UL
Park Keeper/Grounds Staff	Entry /1		Sciences		WAD

Job title	Minimum entry level	Essential GCSEs	Useful subjects	Other academic / training requirements	CLCI reference
Veterinary Nurse	1/2	4 including English Language and Maths or Science to qualify for the Royal College of Veterinary Surgeons Veterinary Nursing Scheme	Science/Biology		WAL
Veterinary Surgeon	4	Good spread	English, Maths, Double Science (or equivalent)	Veterinary degree is essential – this requires very good science A-levels	WAL
Zoo Keeper	Entry/1/2	No set requirements, but good GCSEs helpful	English, Maths, Science, Geography, a foreign language, practical subjects	None before entry	WAM

Useful websites

Careers with Horses – www.equiworld.net/abrs
– www.bhs.org.uk/

Environment – www.environmentjob.co.uk/
Environment and Land-based Industries – www.lantra.co.uk
Horticulture – www.ca.courses-careers.com/horticulture.htm
Veterinary Surgeon – www.rcvs.org.uk/visitors/vetcareers/careersinfo.html

I'm Thinking About a Career in . . . Financial Services (I)

Job title	Minimum entry level	Essential GCSEs	Useful subjects	Other academic/training requirements	CLCI reference
Accountant (Chartered, Management, Public Service)	2/3/4	5 including Maths, English	Business Studies/ Economics, Modern Foreign Languages	A-levels or equivalent, Degree	NAB
Accounting Technician	1/2	English, Maths	Business Studies/ Economics, ICT		NAB
Actuary	3/4	5 including English, Maths	Statistics, Business Studies/Economics	A-levels or equivalent	NAB
Bank/Building Society/ Insurance Clerk	1/2	English, Maths	Modern Languages, Business Studies/ Economics, ICT		NAD NAF NAG
Banker/Bank or Building Society Manager	2/3/4	English, Maths	Modern Foreign Languages, Business Studies/Economics, ICT	A-levels or Degree	NAD NAF
Insurance Broker/ Underwriter	2/3/4	4 including English, Maths	Business Studies/ Economics	BTEC National Diploma, A-levels, Degree	NAG
Insurance Salesman/woman	2	4 including English, Maths	Business Studies/ Economics	A-levels, Degree	NAG
Investment Analyst	4	5 including English, Maths	Statistics, Business Studies/Economics	A-levels or Degree	NAL
Stockbroker	2/3/4	5 including English, Maths	Business Studies/ Economics, ICT, Modern Languages, Geography, Science	A-levels or Degree	NAL

Useful websites

Accountancy – www.aia.org.uk/Careers_in_Accountancy/careers_in_accountancy.html
– www.insidecareers.co.uk/inca.nsf/homepage?openpage

Accounting Technicians – www.aat.co.uk
Financial Services – www.fsnto.org
Insurance – www.cii.co.uk

I'm Thinking About a Career in . . . Healthcare (J)

Job title	Minimum entry level	Essential GCSEs	Useful subjects	Other academic / training requirements	CLCI reference
Ambulance Staff	Entry/1	4 including English, Maths, Science			JOC
Beautician/Beauty Therapist	Entry/1/2/3/4	3 including English, Science		College course after GCSEs or A-levels	IK
Care Assistant	Entry/1/2/3		Home Economics, English, Social Sciences	Care/Social Work course, NVQ training	KEB
Chiropodist	3/4	5 including English, Double Science (or equivalent)		2 A-levels (preferably Science) then full-time NVQ training	JAT
Chiropractor	4	5 including English, Double Science		3 A-levels (sciences) then full-time NVQ training	JOD
Dental Hygienist	2/3	5 including English Language, Science		Experience as dental surgery assistant	JAF
Dental Nurse	Entry/1/2/3	2–4 including English, Science		Full-time course sometimes available	JAF
Dental Technician	2/3	4 including English, Maths, Science	Practical/technical subjects	Possibly full-time course	JAF
Dentist	4	Maths, Double Science (or equivalent), English Language		Science A-levels, Dentistry degree	JAF
Dietitian	4	5 including English, Double Science, Maths Food Studies	Home Economics/	2 A-levels (Chemistry and another Science) or BTEC National Diploma/ Certificate/SVQ2 in Science, Degree in Dietetics	JAV

			Practical subjects	Possibly full-time NVQ training	
Dispensing Optician	2/3	5 including English, Maths, Science		Possibly full-time NVQ training	JAL
Doctor	4	English, Maths, Double Science		3 A-levels in Maths/Science subjects, Medical degree	JAB
Hairdresser	Entry/1		English, Art, Maths, Science	College course, Modern Apprenticeship or NVQ training	IL
Home Economist	3/4	3–4 including English, Maths, Science	Maths, Home Economics/Food Studies	Diploma/Higher Diploma, Degree	ID
Hospital Nurse	2/3/4	5 including English, Maths, Science	Home Economics/Food Studies	A-levels, Pre-Nursing/Health Care course	JAD
Hospital Porter	Entry/1		English, Maths, Science		JOZ
Medical Technical Officer	2/3/4	4 including English, Maths, Double Science	A-levels (sciences), Higher National Diploma, Degree		JOB
Nursing Auxiliary	Entry/1		Home Economics/Food Studies, Science		JAD
Occupational Therapist	4	5 including English, Maths, Science	Maths, practical subjects	2 A-levels (sciences preferred), Degree in Occupational Therapy	JAR
Operating Department Assistant	Entry/1		English, Maths, Science		JOZ
Optician	4	5 including English, Maths, Double Science (or equivalent)		2 A-levels (Maths and science subjects), Degree in Optometry/Ophthalmics	JAL

Job title	Minimum entry level	Essential GCSEs	Useful subjects	Other academic / training requirements	CLCI reference
Orthoptist	4	5 including English, Maths, Science		2 A-levels (Science), Orthoptics Degree	JAL
Osteopath	4	5 including English, Double Science		2 A-levels (Sciences), full-time NVQ training. Qualified doctor to train at London College of Osteopathic Medicine	JOD
Pharmacist	4			A-levels including Chemistry, Pharmacy Degree	JAG
Pharmacy Technician	2	3–4 including English, Maths, Science			JAG
Physiological Measurement Technician (e.g. Cardiology, Audiology etc.)	2/3	4 including English, Maths, Double Science	Technical/practical subjects	2 Science A-levels	JOB
Physiotherapist	4	5 including English, Maths, Double Science		2 A-levels including Biology, Degree in Physiotherapy	JAN
Radiographer	4	5 including English, Maths, Double Science		2 Science A-levels, Degree at School of Radiography	JAP
Speech/Language Therapist	4	5 including English	Maths, Modern Foreign Languages	2 Science A-levels, Degree	JAS

Useful website

Health and Medicine – www.nhscareers.nhs.uk/

I'm Thinking About a Career in . . . Languages, Information and Culture (K)

Job title	Minimum entry level	Essential GCSEs	Useful subjects	Other academic/training requirements	CLCI reference
Archaeologist	4		English, History, Classical Languages, Science	A-levels, Degree	FAH
Archivist	4	English	Modern and Classical Languages, History	A-levels, Degree	FAG
Interpreter/Translator	4	English, 2 Modern Foreign Languages	Classical Languages	Languages Degree	FAL
Librarian/Information Officer	4	English, Maths, Modern Foreign Language	ICT	A-levels, Degree	FAF
Library Assistant/Information Assistant	2/3	4–5 including English, ICT Maths		BTEC National Diploma, A-levels	FAF
Museum Assistant	2/3	4 including English	Art/Design subjects	A-levels, Degree	FAE
Museum Conservation Technician	2/3/4	English	Science, History, craft subjects	A-levels, Degree	FAE

Useful websites

Cultural Industries – www.metier.org.uk
Interpreter/Translator – www.cilt.org.uk/
Librarian/Information Management – www.cilip.org.uk/jobs_careers/employ.html
Museum, Gallery and Heritage Work – www.chnto.co.uk/training/index.html
Scientific and Technical Communicators – www.istc.org.uk

I'm Thinking About a Career in . . . Legal and Political Services (L)

Job title	Minimum entry level	Essential GCSEs	Useful subjects	Other academic/training requirements	CLCI reference
Barrister	4	5 including English	History, Modern Foreign Languages	Arts/Social Science A-levels, Degree	LAB
Barrister's Clerk	2/3/4	4 including English, Maths	ICT		LZ
Legal Executive	2/3	4 including English and academic subjects	Business Studies	A-levels	LAD
Legal Secretary	2/3	3–4 including English	Business Studies, ICT	Secretarial course, A-levels	LAZ
Solicitor	4	5 including English	Modern Foreign Languages, History	Arts/Social Science A-levels, Law Degree	LAC

Useful websites

Barrister & Solicitor – www.lawcareers.net
– www.lawsociety.net

I'm Thinking About a Career in . . . Leisure, Sport and Tourism (M)

Job title	Minimum entry level	Essential GCSEs	Useful subjects	Other academic/training requirements	CLCI reference
Professional Sportsman/ Woman	Entry /1				GAG
Resort Representative	1/2/3/4		English, Maths, Geography, Languages	NVQs	GAX
Sport and Leisure Centre Assistant	1/2/3		English, Maths, Science	BTEC or A-levels	GAJ
Sports/Leisure Centre Manager	2/3/4	5 including English, Maths	Science, Business Studies	BTEC National, Degree	GAJ
Travel Agent	2/3/4	4 including English, Maths	Modern Languages, Geography, Business Studies, ICT	Modern Apprenticeship or A-levels, Degree	GAX
Travel Courier/Resort Representative	1/2/3	Modern Languages	English, Maths, Geography	A-levels	GAX

Useful websites

Leisure Industry (including Sports/Leisure Centre work) – www.ilam.co.uk/pd-careers.asp
Sport – news.bbc.co.uk/sportacademy/hi/sa/learning_centre/careers/default.stm
Travel and Tourism – www.springboarduk.org.uk/
Tourism – www.tourismskillsnetwork.org.uk/local/careersintourism

I'm Thinking About a Career in . . . Manufacturing and Production (N)

Job title	Minimum entry level	Essential GCSEs	Useful subjects	Other academic/training requirements	CLCI reference
Baker	Entry/1/2/3	English, Maths, Science	Home Economics	BTEC National Diploma course	SAC
Factory Worker (skilled)	1	2–3	Maths, Science, Design & Technology/practical subjects		SAB
Factory Worker (unskilled or semi-skilled)	Entry /1		Practical/craft subjects		SAB
Food Processing Worker	Entry 1/			Modern Apprenticeship/ NVQ training	SAC
Foundry Worker	Entry		Practical/Craft subjects, Design & Technology		SAM
Industrial Technician (e.g. Polymers, Brewing, Textiles, Photographic)	2	4–5 including English, Maths, Science	Design & Technology/ Engineering, practical subjects, ICT	BTEC National	S/SAN SAC SAG/EV
Industrial Technologist (e.g. Printing, Textiles, Food, Packaging)	4	Maths, Science, English		A-levels (Science/Maths), Higher National Diploma, Degree	S/SAR/ AG/SAP/ QON
Packer	Entry /1		Practical Subjects		SAB

Production Manager	3/4	4–5 including English, Maths, Science	Engineering/Design & Technology, ICT, Business Studies/ Economics	A-levels, Degree (Science/ Engineering/Business)	ROD
Sewing Machinist/ Milliner	Entry /1		Home Economics (dress and fabrics)	Modern Apprenticeship/ NVQ training	SAH
Woodworking Machinist/ Furniture Makers	Entry /1	Maths, Design & Technology	Practical/craft subjects		UF

Useful websites

Engineering Manufacture – www.semta.org.uk

I'm Thinking About a Career in . . . Marketing and Advertising (O)

Job title	Minimum entry level	Essential GCSEs	Useful subjects	Other academic / training requirements	CLCI reference
Advertising Executive	3/4	English, Maths	Art/Design subjects, Social Sciences, Business Studies/Economics	A-levels, Degree	OD
Advertising Copywriter	3/4	5 including English	Art/Design subjects, Social Sciences	2 A-levels, Diploma, Degree	OD
Estate Agent/Auctioneer	2/3/4	4–5 including English, Maths	Science, Business Studies/Economics	A-levels, Diploma, Degree	UM
Market Researcher Interviewer	1/2	English, Maths			OB
Marketing Manager	4	4 including English, Maths	Business Studies/Economics, Modern Languages, Social Sciences	A-levels or BTEC/SVQ, Business Studies/Marketing Degree or HND/HNC	OB
Marketing Research Executive	3/4	5 including English, Maths	Business Studies/Economics, Modern Languages, Science, Statistics, Social Sciences	A-levels, Degree	OB
Purchasing/Buying Assistant	2	4–5 including English, Maths	Business Studies/Economics, ICT		OP

Purchasing Officer/ Buyer	2/3/4	4–5 including English, Business Studies/ Economics, ICT Maths	A-levels, Degree, Business Studies qualification	OP
Retail Manager	2/3/4	4–5 including English, Business Studies/ Economics Maths	A-levels, BTEC/SVQ, Degree	OE
Sales Representative/ Manager	1/2	English, Maths	A-levels, Degree	OM OE
Shop Assistant/Shelf Filler/ Cashier	Entry/1	English, Maths		OE
Telephone Sales Clerk	1/2	English, Maths		OM

Useful website

Advertising – www.adassoc.org.uk

I'm Thinking About a Career in . . . Media, Print and Publishing (P)

Job title	Minimum entry level	Essential GCSEs	Useful subjects	Other academic/training requirements	CLCI reference
Author	Entry/1/2/3/4		English, ICT		FAC
Journalist	2/3/4	5 including English	ICT	A-levels, pre-entry course, Modern Apprenticeship, Degree	FAC
Machine Printer	2/3	English, Maths		Modern Apprenticeship	SAH
Multimedia Designer	2/3/4	English, Maths, ICT or Science		HND/HNC or Degree	CAV
Originator	1/2/3/4		English, Art, Design, ICT	Modern Apprenticeship	SAH
Print Finisher/Bookbinder	2/3	4 GCSEs	Art, Design & Technology	Modern Apprenticeship	SAH
Publicity Officer/Public Relations Officer	4	English		A-levels, Degree, training in Journalism	OG
Publisher/Editor	3/4	English	Maths, Design subjects	A-levels, Diploma, Degree	FAD

Useful websites

Audio Visual Industries – www.skillset.org
Journalism – www.newspapersoc.org.uk
Printing – www.bpif.org.uk

I'm Thinking About a Career in . . . Performing Arts (Q)

Job title	Minimum entry level	Essential GCSEs	Useful subjects	Other academic/training requirements	CLCI reference
Actor/Actress	Entry/1/2/3/4/5		English Literature, Drama, Music	A-levels, Degree	GAB
Box Office Staff	Entry /1	Maths	Office Skills		GAB
Camera-Man/Woman/Camera Operator	2	3 including English, Maths, Science (Physics)	Technical subjects		GAL
Dancer	Entry/1/2/3/4	5	Music, Drama	A-levels, Degree	GAF
Fashion/Photographic Model	Entry /1	3	Drama	London College of Fashion course	OT
Film Editor (TV)	3/4	Maths, Science	Art, Drama	A-levels, Film course	GAL
Film Producer	Entry/1/2/3/4		English		GAL
Floor/Stage Manager	1/2/3/4/5		Art, Design & Technology, Drama, English, English Literature	Pre-entry courses, Degree	GAT
Lighting Technician (Theatre)	1/2/3	Science, Maths, Design & Technology	Art, Drama	Electrician Training, Theatre Lighting course	GAT
Make-up Artist	2/3/4	English, Art	Science, History, Drama	Hairdressing, Beauty Therapy, A-levels	GAL/GAT
Singer/Musician	Entry/1/2/3/4		Music, Drama	Music college training, A-levels	GAD

Job title	Minimum entry level	Essential GCSEs	Useful subjects	Other academic/training requirements	CLCI reference
Sound Technician/ Operator (Film/TV)	2/3/4	3 including English Language, Maths, Science	Technical subjects	BTEC Certificate or Diploma at National or Higher Level, BA Music Tonmeister	GAL
Stage Designer	4	Art & Design subjects	Drama	Theatre/Stage Design course, A-levels	GAT
Studio Manager (Radio)	4	English, Science	Practical subjects	Experience in sound recording or radio	GAL

Useful websites

Acting – www.drama.ac.uk/careers.html
Audio Visual Industries – www.skillset.org/
Singer/Musician – www.ism.org
Stage Technician – www.abtt.org.uk

I'm Thinking About a Career in . . . Personal and Cleaning Support Services (R)

Job title	Minimum entry level	Essential GCSEs	Useful subjects	Other academic / training requirements	CLCI reference
Beautician/Beauty Therapist	Entry/1/2/3/4	3 including English, Science		College course after GCSEs or A-levels	IK
Chiropodist	3/4	5 including English, Double Science (or equivalent)		2 A-levels (preferably Science) then full-time NVQ training	JAT
Hairdresser	Entry/1		English, Art, Maths, Science	College course, Modern Apprenticeship or NVQ training	IL
Hospital Porter	Entry/1		English, Maths, Science		JOZ

Useful websites

Beautician/Beauty therapist – www.ca.courses-careers.com/therapy.htm
Chiropodist – www.nhscareers.nhs.uk/careers/ahp/chi01_index.html
Hospital Porter – www.learndirect-advice.co.uk/helpwithyourcareer/jobprofiles/profiles/profile179/

I'm Thinking About a Career in . . . Retail Sales and Customer Services (S)

Job title	Minimum entry level	Essential GCSEs	Useful subjects	Other academic / training requirements	CLCI reference
Butcher	Entry/1/2		English, Maths, Science	NVQ in Meat Processing or Modern Apprenticeship	OFM
Call Centre Operator/ Telephone Sales	1/2	English, Maths		NVQ in Telesales or City & Guilds in Call Centre Operations	OM
Estate Agent/Auctioneer	2/3/4	4–5 including English, Maths	Science, Business Studies/Economics	A-levels, Diploma, Degree	UM
Purchasing/Buying Assistant	2	4–5 including English, Maths	Business Studies/ Economics, ICT		OP
Purchasing Officer/ Buyer	2/3/4	4–5 including English, Maths	Business Studies/ Economics, ICT	A-levels, Degree, Business Studies qualification	OP
Retail Manager	2/3/4	4–5 including English, Maths	Business Studies/ Economics	A-levels, BTEC/SVQ, Degree	OE
Sales Representative/ Manager	1/2	English, Maths		A-levels, Degree	OM OE
Shop Assistant/Shelf Filler/ Cashier	Entry/1	English, Maths			OE

Useful websites

Purchasing and Supply – www.cips.org
Retail – www.skillsmart.com/default.asp

I'm Thinking About a Career in . . . Science, Mathematics and Statistics (T)

Job title	Minimum entry level	Essential GCSEs	Useful subjects	Other academic/training requirements	CLCI reference
Biologist/ Biochemist	3/4	5 including English, Maths, Science	Statistics	Science A-levels, Science Degree	QOD
Environmental Scientist/ Ecologist	4	English, Maths, Science	Geography, Geology	Science/Maths A-levels, Degree	QOL
Geologist/Geophysicist	4	English, Maths, Science	Engineering/Technology subjects, Geography, Geology	Science/Maths A-levels, Degree	QOL
Industrial Chemist/ Food Scientist/ Pharmaceuticals Scientist	3/4	5 including English, Maths, Science	Modern Languages	Science A-levels, Science Degree	SAV/ QON
Information Scientist	4	English, Maths, Science, Modern Languages	ICT	A-levels, Degree	FAF
Laboratory Technician	2/3	4 including Maths, Science	English, ICT	A-levels, Diploma	QOX/ JAX/FAB
Mathematician/Statistician	4	English, Maths	Science, Business Studies/Economics, ICT	Maths A-level(s), Degree	QOG/ QOJ
Metallurgist/Materials Scientist	4	English, Maths, Science	Engineering/Technology subjects	Science/Maths A-levels, Metallurgy/Materials Science Degree	QOS

Job title	Minimum entry level	Essential GCSEs	Useful subjects	Other academic / training requirements	CLCI reference
Meteorologist	4	English, Maths, Science	ICT, Astronomy	Science/Maths A-levels, BTEC/SVQ, Physics/ Maths/Meteorology Degree	QOL
Physicist/Astronomer/ Astrophysicist	4	English, Maths, Science	Engineering/Technology subjects, Astronomy, ICT	Science/Maths A-levels, Degree	QOF
Technical Writer	4	English, Maths, Science	Design/Technology, ICT	A-levels, Science/Engineering subject Degree	FAC

Useful websites

Chemistry – www.chemsoc.org
Microbiology – www.socgenmicrobiol.org.uk
Environmental Scientist/Ecologist – www.environmentjob.co.uk/
Geologist/Geophysicist – www.geolsoc.org.uk
Metallurgist/Materials Scientist – www.iom3.org/
Physics and Engineering in Medicine – www.ipem.org.uk

I'm Thinking About a Career in . . . Security and Armed Forces (U)

Job title	Minimum entry level	Essential GCSEs	Useful subjects	Other academic/training requirements	CLCI reference
Army – Soldiers and Service Women	Entry/1/2		Maths, Science, Design & Technology	None before entry	BAF
Army Officer	2/3/4/5		English, Maths and Science or a Modern Foreign Language	Most opportunities require at least 2 A-levels and/or a degree	B/BAF
Firefighter/Fire Officer	Entry/1/2	English, Maths, Science	Practical subjects	Modern Apprenticeship	MAF
Police Constable	Entry/1/2		English	None before entry	MAB
Police Officer	Entry/1/2/3/4	4 including English, Maths	Social Sciences	A-levels, Degree	MAB
Prison Governor	4	English	Social Sciences	Social Sciences/Psychology A-levels, Degree	MAD
Prison Officer	Entry/1/2	English	Social Sciences	None before entry	MAD
RAF Airman/Woman	Entry/1/2	Maths, Science and preferably English	Sciences	None before entry	BAL
RAF Officer	3/4	Minimum of 5 including English Language and Maths	Science	A-levels and/or higher diploma/degree	B/BAL
Royal Marines – Other Ranks	Entry/1/2		Selection test involves reasoning, English Language, Numeracy and Mechanical comprehension	None before entry	BAB

Job title	Minimum entry level	Essential GCSEs	Useful subjects	Other academic/training requirements	CLCI reference
Royal Navy/WRNS Ratings	Entry/1/2	Technical specialisms require 1, 2 or more including English, Maths and a Science Medical technicians require 5.	Medical technicians Scientific and technical/ practical subjects	None before entry	BAB
Royal Navy and Royal Marines Officer	2/3/4	5 including English and Maths	Science, Languages	A-levels normally required; graduate entry also available	B/BAB
Security Officer	Entry/1/2		English, Maths and practical subjects	Modern Apprenticeship possible	MAG

Useful websites

Army – www.army.mod.uk/careers/
Firefighter/Fire Officer – www.lgcareers.com/careers/profile.asp?83
Police Work – www.police.uk
RAF – www.raf.mod.uk
Royal Navy and Marines – www.royal-navy.mod.uk

I'm Thinking About a Career in . . . Social Work and Counselling Services (V)

Job title	Minimum entry level	Essential GCSEs	Useful subjects	Other academic/training requirements	CLCI reference
Careers/Personal Adviser	4	5 including English	Social Sciences	Usually A-levels and degree, then qualification in Career Guidance or NVQ in Guidance or Advice, Guidance and Advocacy	KED
Charities Manager/Organiser	3/4	5 including English	Maths, Business Studies, Social Sciences	A-levels, Degree, Social Work training	KEM
Educational Psychologist	4	Maths, English	Science, Social Sciences, Statistics	A-levels, Psychology Degree, Teaching requirements	KEL
Health Visitor	2/3/4	5 including English, Maths, Science	Home Economics/Food Studies, Social Sciences	WRNS Nurse Training, Health Visitor's Course, A-levels	JAD JAD
Probation Officer	4	5 including English, Maths	Social Sciences, Statistics	A-levels, Diploma in Social Work	KEB
Psychologist/ Psychotherapist	4	5 including English, Maths	Science, Social Sciences, Statistics	A-levels, Degree	KEL
Religious Ministry (Priest, Minister etc.)	1/2/3/4		English, Religious Studies, History	A-levels, Degree, Theological Training	FAM
Residential Care Assistant (e.g.Homes for Elderly)	Entry/1/2/3		English, Home Economics, Social Sciences	College course in a Care subject or pre-social work	KEB

Job title	Minimum entry level	Essential GCSEs	Useful subjects	Other academic/training requirements	CLCI reference
Residential Social Worker	4	4–5 including English	Social Sciences	A-levels, Diploma in Social Work	KEB
Social Worker	4	5 including English, Maths	Statistics, Social Sciences	A-levels, Diploma in Social Work	KEB
Youth and Community Worker	4	5 including English	Social Sciences	A-levels, Diploma, Degree	KEG

Useful websites

Careers/Personal Adviser – www.prospects.ac.uk/downloads/occprofiles/profile_pdfs/B2_Careers_adviser_personal_adviser_(careers).pdf
Charities/Voluntary Organisation Work – www.ncvo-vol.org.uk/asp/search/ncvo/main.aspx?siteID=1
Drug & Alcohol Youth Worker – www.lgcareers.com/careers/profile.asp?186
Health Visitor – www.careers-gateway.co.uk/links/index/06/0632.htm
Psychologist/Psychotherapist – www.bps.org.uk/index.cfm
Social Worker – www.socialworkcareers.co.uk

I'm Thinking About a Career in . . . Transport and Logistics (W)

Job title	Minimum entry level	Essential GCSEs	Useful subjects	Other academic/training requirements	CLCI reference
Air Cabin Crew	2/3	Modern Languages, English, Maths	Geography, Home Economics/Food Studies	A-levels, experience in Nursing, Care Work, Catering	YAB
Driver (Bus, Taxi, Lorry etc.)	Entry /1		Motor Vehicle Studies	Car driving licence pre-entry	YAD
Merchant Navy Deck Officer	3/4	4 including Maths, Science, English	Nautical Studies, Design/Technology, Geography	Maths/Science A-levels, Degree	YAL
Merchant Navy Deck/ Catering Rating	1	3 including Maths, Science, English		Nautical Studies, Home Economics/ Food Studies	YAL
Merchant Navy Engineering Officer	2/3/4	4 including Maths, Science, English	Nautical Studies, Design/Technology	Maths/Physics A-levels, Degree	YAL
Railway Fitter/Electrician	1/2	English, Maths, Science	Design/Technology, Engineering		YAF
Road Transport Manager	3/4	5 including English, Maths	Economics, Business Studies, ICT	A-levels, Degree	YAD

Useful websites

Merchant Navy – www.mntb.org/careers/companies.htm
Railway Industry – www.careersinrail.org
Road Transport Manager/Logistics & Transport – www.iolt.org.uk/pages/home

11. How has GCSE worked in practice?

How do GCSE results compare with the old system?
Generally, very favourably. The overall pattern is one of higher standards, although reservations about some aspects of the examination and its assessment procedures have led to some of the changes described in this book.

The Government uses GCSE (and equivalent) achievement as its principal way of measuring improvement in teaching and learning for 15- to 16-year-olds.

The Government has set the following KS4 targets for 2004:

- Increase by 4 percentage points from 2002 the number of students achieving five or more GCSE grades A*–C (or equivalent), with at least 38 per cent achieving this standard in every LEA.
- No school has fewer than 20 per cent of students aged 16 achieving five higher grades at GCSE.
- 92 per cent of 16-year-olds to obtain five or more GCSEs at grades A*–G including English and Mathematics.

The percentage of students receiving good grades at GCSE is improving: there was a 1.3 percentage point increase to 52.9 per cent of students gaining five or more grades A*–C (or the GNVQ equivalent) in 2003.

The number of schools with less than 20 per cent of students achieving five or more A*–C grades has fallen by two-thirds since 1997.

The percentage of students achieving no passes fell further in 2003 to 5.2 per cent.

Is it true that girls do better than boys?

YES. The main barrier to meeting the targets has been underachievement by boys. Girls continue to outperform boys, particularly at the higher grades, although the difference narrowed slightly in 2003. 57.8 per cent of girls got five A*–C grades, compared to 47.5 per cent of boys.

How will I get my results?

Each awarding body is responsible for publishing the results of its examinations on a jointly agreed date, usually towards the end of August.

The results will be sent to your school or college who will then forward them to you. Some schools and colleges make arrangements for candidates to collect their results in person. Your school or college will always tell you the date on which you can expect to receive or collect them.

How can I be sure that my grade will be accurate?

Proven inaccuracies have been very few, considering the millions of subject entries. Remember that the system of checking marking and results includes impartial observers and that the checking system is *very* thorough.

There are six levels of enquiry service provided by the awarding bodies, ranging from a quick clerical check to a full re-mark and report. Barely half a per cent of all GCSE candidates make an enquiry, either individually or through their schools.

If you do wish to use the appeals system to query your GCSE grade, in the first instance you should appeal to your school or college. If they think a mistake has been made, they will put in an appeal to the awarding body on your behalf. Private candidates can make independent enquiries direct to the board. It costs about £15 for an exam script to be re-examined, but schools are reimbursed if they win their case. The school has to submit any such results enquiry to the relevant awarding body within about four weeks of the results being published.

If the school or centre is not satisfied with the outcome of an enquiry, it can submit a formal appeal to the awarding body. Then there is yet another stage if the school or centre is still dissatisfied with the outcome. An Examinations Appeals Board (EAB) was set up in 1999. Its role is to help ensure that candidates, parents, schools and colleges are satisfied that the grades awarded are fair and as accurate as possible. The EAB only becomes involved when the awarding bodies' own procedures have been exhausted.

In Northern Ireland, the CCEA is unique in offering an accelerated service which re-marks papers within two weeks for an extra fee.

In Scotland, anyone can query results, though not everyone can instigate the formal appeal. The Scottish system had a major setback in summer 2000, when flaws in a new SQA computer system meant that 4,000 candidates received incomplete or inaccurate Standard grade results. Considerable efforts have been made to ensure that there is no repetition of this mishap.

If an appeal goes the wrong way, could I get a lower grade?

Yes. Until the year 2001, candidates awarded a GCSE (or A-level) subject grade had their initial result protected if they were subsequently included in an enquiry or appeal – their grade could be raised but not lowered. The rules have now changed. Where a clerical check or re-mark of an externally assessed paper reveals inaccurate marking, subject grades may now be lowered, raised or confirmed. This is seen as being the approach that is fairest to *all* candidates.

There are certain circumstances in which subject grades remain protected:

1. In cases where a re-moderation of internally assessed work reveals inaccurate assessment. Here, marks gained in a module, unit or component may be lowered, raised or confirmed, but subject grades may only be confirmed or raised.
2. On rare occasions when an awarding body has a concern about a particular examiner's accuracy which only emerges after results have been issued. Here, work is re-marked without the prior consent of candidates. Consequently, subject grades of candidates involved in this process will not be lowered.

In summary, it is now even more important to think twice before considering the appeals process. Remember that your teachers are in a good position to make an accurate assessment of your work. The likelihood of an error in the marking remains very low.

How do I know that the system really is fair?

The DfES is actively encouraging more openness in the examining body procedures. It wants to see greater freedom of information, improved accountability and clearer feedback to schools. From 2000, candidates in English, Irish, Welsh and Mathematics were able to request access to their own scripts. This access has now been extended to all GCSE subjects. Requests have to be made through the school or examination centre (with private candidates able to arrange access direct through the relevant awarding body). Such requests have to be made by early October, with the schools (or centres) receiving the papers in the period late September to mid-November.

Schools also have an independent right to request scripts, in order to support staff in their teaching, but candidates have the right to prevent their schools requesting their scripts by writing to the headteacher.

Schools can also request photocopies of re-marked scripts, along with the outcome of enquiries on results for GCSE scripts involved in the access scheme (covering English, Irish, Welsh and Mathematics).

The awarding bodies also provide revision guidance through broadcasters and the media, along with past papers, student guides and exam resources on the web. They support teachers through a range of materials, including teachers' guides, coursework guides, examiner reports, videos, tapes and classroom delivery materials.

The awarding bodies also provide a vast annual in-service education and training programme covering current and new specifications – with opportunities for teachers to participate in trial marking and to ask questions of senior examiners and specification developers.

Has GCSE really proved suitable for all?

GCSE is open to anyone at school or college, whatever their ability. However, it is not always the right course or qualification for some less able students. This is because of the high requirement for literacy and the demands of coursework.

It is difficult to provide courses and exams that will suit the whole age group. An increasing number of courses are being provided for students who are unlikely to achieve a GCSE grade G or an equivalent qualification (Foundation GNVQ or NVQ level 1).

Entry Level is the first level of the National Qualifications Framework. It is below Foundation level and is itself divided into three sub-levels: 1, 2 and 3, which are broadly equivalent to National Curriculum levels 1, 2 and 3.

There are Entry Level Certificates in:

- the subjects that students will have studied up to the age of 14; as well as
- broader vocational areas that are more like GCSEs in vocational subjects.

For a full list of Entry Level qualifications available, see 'What subjects are available?' below.

Where does Entry Level fit?

In maintained schools, Entry Level qualifications are intended to be used by compulsory school age pupils with special needs whose attainment level falls below GCSE grade G in one or more subject areas.

Students can take Entry Level Certificates alongside GCSEs, GNVQs (until they are phased out), GCSEs in vocational subjects or NVQs. They are assessed in tasks which may be written, spoken or practical.

Entry level provides a common progression route to GCSE, GNVQ and NVQ qualifications.

For those working below National Curriculum or Entry Level 1, there is an opportunity to achieve units of Entry Level qualifications. They can also work on programmes of study that lead to school- or college-based (rather than national) certification.

What subjects are available?

Subject areas available include:

- Art
- Art and Design

- Art and Design (Fine Art)
- Art and Design (Graphic Design)
- Art and Design (Photography)
- Art and Design (Textiles)
- Art and Design (3D Design)
- Business Language Competence
- Business Studies
- Catering
- Child Development
- Childcare
- Design & Technology (Electronic Products)
- Design & Technology (Food Technology)
- Design & Technology (Graphic Products)
- Design & Technology (Resistant Materials Technology)
- Design & Technology (Systems & Control Technology)
- Design & Technology (Textiles Technology)
- English
- Food Studies
- French
- Geography
- German
- Graphical & Material Studies
- Hairdressing
- History
- Home Economics
- Humanities
- ICT
- Job-seeking Skills
- Land Studies
- Learning Skills
- Leisure and Tourism
- Life Skills
- Manufacturing
- Materials Technology
- Mathematics
- Media Studies
- Motor Vehicle and Road User Studies
- Music
- Office Practice

- Physical Education
- Preparation for Employment
- Religious Studies
- Retail
- Science
- Skills for Working Life
- Spanish
- Textiles
- Travel and Tourism
- Welsh
- Welsh Second Language.

Most courses have been developed by the main awarding bodies, with a few local syllabuses also approved by the regulatory authorities.

Your school will be able to tell you whether it is operating any of these alternatives.

How are Entry Level awards assessed?
At Entry Level, much of the assessment is done through teacher-marked tests.

What advice can you give me on which level of exam to choose?
In subjects where there is a choice of level, you must first of all listen to the advice of your subject teachers. Try to resist the temptation to disregard what they say just because the alternative option holds out the possibility of a higher – or safer – grade. They are probably the best judges of your potential.

What difference has GCSE made to the way my subjects are taught?
Most importantly, it has raised standards of teaching. Her Majesty's Inspectorate (HMI) visits to schools have indicated a significant improvement in the standard of lessons observed.

In particular, the HMIs found that study for the new exam has raised both students' motivation and performance, and teaching quality. They stated that 'teachers appear to have become more aware of what [students] are capable of achieving'.

GCSE has led to a marked improvement in oral and written work, and more and better practical and investigative work. It has increased the ability of students to show what they know, understand and can do, especially in their coursework. The additional emphasis given to positive achievement in both coursework and the exams is probably the greatest success of GCSE.

Will GCSE prepare me for study at higher level?
GCSE has had a positive impact on the numbers of young people staying on in full-time education in order to take AS and A-levels or equivalent courses.

AS and A-levels themselves have begun to change and are likely to be revised further, partly to reflect the differences in the GCSE syllabuses. In a more positive sense, they should also change in order to take maximum benefit from the new skills being measured by the GCSE.

Remember that you need to do *really well* in a subject at GCSE to consider taking it at AS or A-level. Even a C grade is not a good indicator for AS or A-level success in some subjects. This does *not* mean that you can't take AS or A-levels (or other higher level courses) of which you have no previous experience, as long as this is not simply an 'escape route' and you do have some evidence of your ability to cope.

12. The GCSE in Northern Ireland

In Northern Ireland, the Northern Ireland Council for the Curriculum, Examinations and Assessment (CCEA) advises the Government on curriculum, assessment and examination matters. The CCEA is responsible for conducting Key Stage assessments and the conduct of GCSE and GCE examinations.

The CCEA also regulates standards in GCSE, GCE and GNVQ examinations in Northern Ireland. GCSE syllabuses and examinations in Northern Ireland comply with the GCSE general and subject criteria, taking into account where necessary the distinctive features of the Northern Ireland common curriculum.

The CCEA has recently conducted a review of the Northern Ireland curriculum. The Education Minister has recently announced major forthcoming changes to post-primary education. The key concept of the new arrangements is an Entitlement Framework. This will entitle all pupils and students to access a minimum number and range of courses, including a choice of vocational courses. It should enable young people to keep their options open as long as possible. Some of the changes will not be fully implemented until Autumn 2008.

What will this mean for KS4?
Generally, it should mean that schools will be offering a range of vocational pathways. Age 14 will be the first major decision point for young people to opt towards a vocational pathway. Access to

these pathways is likely to include more collaboration between schools, and between schools and FE colleges. It is also likely that specialist schools will be developed to meet specific local needs.

What GCSE subjects are available in Northern Ireland?
- Additional Mathematics (for post-GCSE Higher Tier students)
- Applied Art & Design*
- Art & Design
- Applied Business*
- Business Studies
- Construction
- Drama
- Economics
- Engineering*
- English
- English Literature
- Financial Services
- French
- Geography
- German
- Health & Social Care*
- History
- Home Economics
- Home Economics: Child Development
- Hospitality
- Applied ICT*
- ICT
- ICT – Short Course
- Irish
- Irish (Gaeilge)
- Journalism
- Learning for Life and Work
- Leisure & Tourism*
- Manufacturing*
- Mathematics
- Motor Vehicle and Road User Studies
- Music
- Physical Education
- Religious Studies

- Religious Studies – Short Course
- Applied Science*
- Science: Biology
- Science: Chemistry
- Science: Double Award
- Science: Physics
- Science: Single Award
- Social and Environmental Studies
- Spanish
- Technology & Design.

* These are the new Double Award vocational courses.

In Northern Ireland the KS4 (Years 11 and 12) curriculum consists of six Areas of Study, six educational (cross-curricular) themes and a course of religious education.

What are these Areas of Study?

The six Areas of Study are:
- English
- Mathematics
- Science and Technology
- The Environment and Society
- Creative and Expressive Studies (Physical Education)
- Language Studies.

Students who have taken GCSE in either English or Mathematics at the end of Year 11 do not have to follow the KS4 programme of study. However, they must take another 'cognate' subject, e.g. English Literature (in the case of English) or Additional Mathematics or Statistics (in the case of Mathematics).

Northern Ireland curriculum programmes of study define the essential content of each subject and are the basis for planning, teaching, learning and assessment objectives. They operate in most Areas of Study. All courses in compulsory subjects which do not have programmes of study now have to be approved by the Department of Education on the advice of CCEA.

In The Environment and Society, there is now a choice of either:
  (a) a course from History/Geography/Business Studies/Home Economics or

(b) an approved course in Economics/Politics or modular provision selected from a range of modules to include Law in our Lives, Environmental Education, Information Technology, Health/Sex Education, Economic Awareness, Cultural Heritage, Careers Education.

Language Studies provision now consists of an approved course, e.g. GCSE or GNVQ unit(s) or Graded Objectives in Modern Languages (GOML).

Will I have much choice?
Reduction in the statutory curriculum time is intended to allow schools further flexibility to meet students' needs. For example, this can be used to provide additional time for the compulsory subjects, to offer additional courses from within the Area of Study framework, or to provide additional elements such as Personal and Social Education and Careers Guidance.

What about coursework?
Coursework weightings are also different in Northern Ireland. The maximum allocations for coursework are as follows:

Additional Mathematics	External assessment only
Applied Art & Design	100%
Art & Design	60%
Applied Business	Two-thirds
Business Studies	20%
Construction	75%
Drama	60%
Economics	External assessment only
Engineering	Two-thirds
English	40%
English Literature	30%
Financial Services	75%
French	External assessment only
Geography	20%
German	External assessment only
Health & Social Care	Two-thirds
History	20%

Home Economics	50%
Home Economics: Child Development	40%
Hospitality	75%
Applied ICT	Two-thirds
ICT	60%
ICT (Short course)	60%
Irish	External assessment
Irish (Gaeilge)	35%
Journalism	75%
Learning for Life and Work	55%
Leisure & Tourism	Two-thirds
Manufacturing	Two-thirds
Mathematics	20%
Motor Vehicle & Road User Studies	40%
Music	75%
Physical Education	70%
Religious Studies	20%
Religious Studies – Short Course	External assessment
Applied Science	Two-thirds
Science: Biology	25%
Science: Chemistry	25%
Science: Double Award	25%
Science: Physics	25%
Science: Single Award	25%
Social and Environmental Studies	Dependent on modules taken
Spanish	External assessment only
Technology & Design	60%

Do we all sit the same exams?

No. There are again tiering arrangements, but these are different in Northern Ireland.

The tiers of entry for Northern Ireland National Curriculum subjects are:

Mathematics	Foundation	D–G
	Intermediate	B–E
	Higher	A*–C

Science	Foundation	C–G
(Double/Single Award)	Higher	A*–D (E)
English Literature	Foundation	C–G (U)
	Higher	A*–E (U)
English	Foundation	C–G
	Higher	A*–D

Other subjects that share the same tiering system as English include: Business Studies, Economics, Geography, Home Economics, ICT (both full and short courses), Irish, all Modern Foreign Languages, Motor Vehicle & Road User Studies, Religious Studies (full course only), and Technology & Design.

Other subjects operate a single tier system.

Important addresses in Northern Ireland
Department of Education Northern Ireland
New St Andrew's House
Balloo Road
Bangor
County Down BT19 2PR
Tel: 028 9127 9279
Website: www.deni.gov.uk

Northern Ireland Council for the Curriculum, Examinations and Assessment
29 Clarendon Road
Clarendon Dock
Belfast BT1 3BG
Tel: 028 9026 1200
Website: www.ccea.org.uk

13. ... And in Scotland

Is the structure of the secondary curriculum and examinations the same as in the rest of the UK?

No. There are several major differences in the Scottish system. Firstly, students in Scotland begin their secondary schooling when they are about 12 years of age. The curriculum is divided into three stages, the first two of which are compulsory. In the first two years of secondary school (S1 and S2), students follow a broad and balanced educational programme. Towards the end of S2, they choose the courses they will study in S3 and S4.

Does this mean that there is more choice for 14- and 15-year-olds in Scotland?

Not entirely. In effect, Scotland has a national curriculum for this age group, since all schools are expected to follow certain guiding principles, as defined by the Scottish Executive and Learning & Teaching Scotland.

The core curriculum is meant to include systematic study within each of the following areas of study:

Language and Communication
Mathematical Studies and Applications
Scientific Studies and Applications
Social and Environmental Studies
Technological Activities and Applications
Creative and Aesthetic Activities
Physical Education
Religious and Moral Education

All Standard Grade courses include one or more of the core skills of Communication, Numeracy, Information Technology, Problem Solving and Working with Others.

What sort of school-leaving examinations are there?
During S3 and S4 most students take Standard Grade courses. Standard Grade is a national programme and the assessments are set and marked by the Scottish Qualifications Authority.

Do I have to take exams in all the different areas of study?
Not as such. The S3 and S4 courses are meant to give each student adequate experience in all the modes, but the S Grade courses are not an exact match to the individual modes. A single course may contribute to several different modes.

Most students take English, Mathematics, *at least* one Science subject, one Social Science subject (e.g. History, Geography, Modern Studies), and one Modern Language.

Students may also choose other subjects from an option list of subjects that the school will provide. They may choose a second subject from one of the 'compulsory' columns, e.g. a second Science or Modern Language, or they may choose a completely different subject, e.g. PE, Music, Religious Education or Drama.

Are all options available in all the schools?
No. Larger schools are normally able to offer a wider choice than smaller schools. National syllabuses also allow schools some flexibility in deciding on course content and on teaching and learning methods. So there may be differences in the teaching of a particular course between one school and another.

How much time will I have to study each subject?
There are recommended minimum and maximum time allocations for each student, based on the assumption that the syllabuses for English and Mathematics would need five 40-minute periods a week and those for other full courses four periods. The normal minimum time requirement (in hours) for each of the modes, over the two-year period, is as follows:

Language and Communication	360
Mathematical Studies and Applications	200

Scientific Studies and Applications	160
Social and Environmental Studies	160
Technological Activities and Applications	80
Creative and Aesthetic Activities	80
Physical Education	80
Religious and Moral Education	80

The total of 1,200 hours allocated to this core of the eight modes represents approximately 70 per cent of the time available to students throughout S3 and S4.

What happens for the rest of the time?

In the remaining 30 per cent of available class time, schools are able to offer a variety of short or modular courses of varying lengths. The most common format for such courses is that of modules leading to the award of the National Certificate by SQA. The SQA modules include a number of courses that serve to complement the curriculum at S3 and S4.

The SQA also provides a limited range of short courses which are certificated on the SQA certificate. These are intended to provide candidates with an extension or enrichment of their curriculum in and after the third year of secondary education. The short courses offered in this way are:

- Classical Studies
- Creative and Aesthetic Studies
- Electronics
- European Studies
- Geology
- Graphic Communication
- Health Studies
- Nautical Studies
- Religious & Moral Education
- Statistics
- Technological Studies.

These short courses which lead to certificated awards are 40-hour units which are internally assessed and externally moderated. Awards are ungraded and are recorded on the same certificate as Standard (or Higher Grade) awards.

Schools can also offer short courses of their own design, which do not lead to national certification.

Are Standard Grade courses and exams the same for all?
Not in all cases. In some areas, such as Mathematics, students follow courses at three levels, i.e. to suit different levels of ability. In other areas, such as English, the course is the same for all, but the skills to be acquired are differentiated to suit the different ability groups.

What is the grading system for the Standard Grade exams?
Standard Grade courses are offered at three levels – Credit (grades 1–2), General (grades 3–4), and Foundation (grades 5–6). The attainment levels are specified by the Grade Related Criteria (GRC), which are available from the Scottish Qualifications Authority (SQA) on request.

Students can take different subjects at different levels, according to their abilities. Many students are taught in joint classes (e.g. General/Foundation), in order to keep Standard Grade options open for as long as possible. Most students actually go on to take examinations covering two pairs of grades, either Credit/General or General/Foundation. This ensures that all students have the best opportunity to gain an award which reflects their real ability and achievement.

A Standard Grade award of grade 3 or better is equivalent to a GCSE award at grade C or better.

What else do I need to know about the assessment system?
It is essentially a performance- or criteria-related method of assessment. In other words, the award is based on the achievements of the individual student, measured against stated standards, rather than on how that individual's achievement compares with that of other candidates.

In order to achieve a particular grade within a particular level, candidates have to give evidence of achievement in all the basic aspects of the subject. For example, in English, candidates will receive separate assessments for Reading, Writing and Talking as well as an overall grade. A Profile of Performance stating all grades then appears on the certificate beside the overall award for the course. To continue the example of English, an individual student's award might therefore be reported in this way:

Subject	Overall Award	Profile of Performance
English	3	Reading 3
		Writing 2
		Talking 4

How will this be assessed?

In a variety of different ways. In most courses, candidates will have to demonstrate attainment in oral or practical skills, and these skills will usually be assessed internally by the class teacher on the basis of work done during the course.

Other aspects, such as Writing in English, will be assessed on the basis of a folio submitted to the SQA, together with a written examination. Others will be assessed through a written examination alone.

In all cases, even where a part of the course is assessed externally, teachers will have submitted estimated grades to the SQA. These can be used to improve the SQA grades in the case of any disagreement.

If an assessment is not available for any part of the course, for whatever reason, no overall grade can be given for the course. The only exception to this is when a candidate is not able to do part of the course because of a particular handicap or impairment.

What about the assessment of short courses?

The individual school is responsible for assessing candidates taking short courses, with the SQA moderating school assessments to ensure national standards.

The SQA certificate then records any short courses which have been completed successfully.

What about the assessment of core skills?

Since the year 2000, the SQA certificate has also listed details of the core skills achieved through success in Standard Grade courses.

Are there any other options at 14+?

Some schools are offering National Qualifications courses and units in S3/S4 in some subjects as an alternative to Standard Grades.

These include courses at Access, Intermediate, Higher and Advanced Higher levels. In S3, you would normally follow Standard Grade, Access or Intermediate courses or units. You may find that you would be doing a mixture of Standard Grades and National Qualifications courses and units.

National Qualifications courses are usually made up of three National units, combined with an end-of-year exam. Each National unit takes about 40 hours to complete and counts as a qualification in its own right.

In addition, some schools may give you the option of getting a Scottish Group Award (SGA) by combining a cluster of National Qualifications courses.

What happens at 16+?

There is a further, optional stage of one or two years for students aged 16 to 18 who wish to stay on at school. At present, most S4 students return to school for S5, where they progress to the new National Qualifications courses for S5 and S6, introduced through the 'Higher Still' reform programme.

What is Higher Still?

It is a new system of post-16 qualifications introduced in Scotland in 1999, administered by the Scottish Qualifications Authority (SQA). The aim of the Higher Still programme is to bring together all existing awards into a single, coherent post-16 system. The new qualifications include National Units, National Courses and Scottish Group Awards (SGAs) and cater for anyone studying after Standard Grade, whether in school or further education college. They are meant to sit alongside and link to Scottish Vocational Qualifications (SVQs).

The new system is based on units, each a qualification in its own right. So, students who pass the units, but not the external examination, still get a national qualification. The units, normally of 40 or 80 hours' teaching time, cover both academic and vocational subjects. Units may be taken on a free-standing basis or grouped together into courses. Units and courses are structured into a series of levels: Access 1, Access 2, Access 3, Intermediate 1 and 2, Higher and Advanced Higher (the last replaces the CSYS).

Standard Grade		Higher Still		SVQs
		Advanced Higher		
		Higher	=	SVQ 3
Credit	=	Intermediate 2	=	SVQ 2
General	=	Intermediate 1	=	SVQ 1
Foundation	=	Access		

How do Standard Grades relate to Higher Still and SVQs?

This means that students who achieve a General pass at Standard Grade normally go on to an Intermediate 2 or SVQ1 or SVQ2. A Foundation pass in Standard Grade can lead to Intermediate 1, although some students may do best to broaden their experience at Access 3 first.

A student who does not manage Standard Grade can attempt Access 2 or 3 units as early as Third Year and progress to additional units at these levels after that, or attempt a Skillstart award.

But these are not firm progression routes and schools will advise students on what subjects and levels they should be considering.

Important addresses in Scotland

Scottish Office Education and Industry Department
Rathgael House
St James Centre
Edinburgh EH1 3SY
Tel: 0131 556 8400
Website: www.scotland.gov.uk

Learning and Teaching Scotland
Glasgow Office
74 Victoria Crescent Road
Glasgow G12 9JN
Tel: 0141 337 5000
Website: www.ltscotland.com

Learning and Teaching Scotland
Dundee Office
Gardyne Road
Dundee DD5 1NY
Tel: 01382 443600
Website: www.ltscotland.com

Scottish Qualifications Authority
Hanover House
24 Douglas Street
Glasgow G2 7NQ
Tel: 0141 242 2214
Website: www.sqa.org.uk

Scottish Credit and Qualifications Framework
Address as for SQA above
Tel: 0141 242 2429
Website: www.scqf.org.uk

Careers Scotland
150 Broomielaw
Atlantic Quay
Glasgow G2 8LU
Careers Scotland
Inverness Retail and Business Park
Inverness IV2 7GF

In this chapter, we have drawn on the information in *Which Way Now? Study Decisions at 14*, produced by Careers Scotland and available online via its website at www.careers-scotland.org.uk.

14. Life after GCSE: options at 16

My options at 16 – how will they affect my choice of GCSEs?
In another two years you will be facing another decision – one that will shape your future. And the choice will be even greater, but you are laying the foundation of that choice now, by choosing your GCSE subjects.

So, before you make your final selection of GCSEs, think carefully about what you might decide to do later on.

The options at 16 are very wide indeed, but these are the major ones.

Getting a job

There's no denying that for some school is just a chore – they can't wait to get out and earn their own living. However, relatively few employers are recruiting at 16. Of those that are, you should certainly be looking more seriously at those offering further training, preferably leading to a National Vocational Qualification. You need to think about what GCSEs would be preferred, or required, to start a job at 16.

Getting a job with NVQ training

You can work with a company or organisation that offers training leading to an NVQ. You would usually attend a college or training centre one day a week, to pick up extra skills that will back up those you are learning in the workplace. This work-based qualification will be related to the skill requirements of the specific job. You will not need any particular qualifications to go onto NVQ Level 1 training. NVQ Level 2 requires GCSEs at grades D–G, while NVQ Level 3 requires 4 GCSEs at grade C or above.

Modern Apprenticeships

Modern Apprenticeships are work-based training programmes, designed for young people who have left full-time education. There are more than 150 types of Modern Apprenticeship available, in over 20 occupational areas of industry and commerce. The Modern Apprenticeship frameworks are specified and certificated by Sector Skills Councils, while the individual qualifications are certificated by Awarding Bodies.

The common elements for each Modern Apprenticeship are:
- an NVQ
- Key Skills
- technical certificates
- enhancements.

They are geared to individual needs and have been very successful in providing high quality training for young people. They are available at two levels. Foundation Modern Apprenticeships provide training to at least NVQ Level 2. Advanced Modern Apprenticeships are for young people training to get at least an NVQ Level 3. Modern Apprentices are also trained in Key Skills, such as team working, communication, IT and problem solving. All candidates beginning Advanced Modern Apprenticeship programmes are now required to achieve at least the Level 2 qualifications in Communication and Application of Number.

Modern Apprenticeships usually last about three years, but can be shorter or longer, depending on several factors, including the occupational area and the level of the programme. They can also lead to further progression and higher qualifications.

Training with a training provider

If jobs with Modern Apprenticeships or NVQ training are not immediately available, a good alternative is to apply for a training place with a local training provider. There will probably be a range of training provider organisations in your area and you can seek information and advice on them from your Connexions Personal Adviser or Careers Adviser. Training providers offer different training opportunities, leading to NVQs and/or Modern Apprenticeships. Whereas you get wages if training as an employee, as a trainee you get a training allowance (and sometimes help with travelling costs).

Delivery of the Modern Apprenticeship is agreed between the learner and the employer. Delivery methods vary depending on the occupational area but may include:

- workplace assessment
- day release at college
- block release at college
- full time at college
- short courses.

Entry qualifications

- Advanced Modern Apprenticeships – five GCSEs grades A*–C or equivalent qualifications or work experience
- Foundation Modern Apprenticeships – GCSE in English and Maths grade E or above or equivalent qualifications or work experience.

In future, it is likely that Modern Apprenticeships will be linked to the diploma system proposed by the Tomlinson Working Group (see Chapter 1, 'Key Stage 4: an overview') and they should eventually be fully integrated into the reformed 14–19 framework.

College courses

Your local college of further education (or tertiary college) is likely to be offering a range of full- and part-time courses. Full-time vocational courses on offer may include GNVQs (while they are still available) and Advanced Vocational A-levels (VCEs), and BTEC/Edexcel First Diploma and National Diploma courses.

The same college may also be offering other courses in competition with, or possibly complementing, the local school sixth form(s), in A/AS levels and GCSEs.

Staying on at school

This will often involve taking AS and A-levels – and now this includes the new VCE A-levels (which replaced Advanced GNVQs). Courses at this level are essential if you want to go on to take a degree.

Post-16, the vocational areas available at VCE are:

- Art and Design
- Business
- Construction and the Built Environment
- Engineering
- Health and Social Care
- Hospitality and Catering
- ICT
- Leisure and Recreation
- Manufacturing
- Media: Communication and Production
- Science
- Travel and Tourism.

If taking A-levels, you'll probably be expected to take four or five subjects over the two-year period, including the new AS level. This new AS qualification is equivalent to the first year of the full A-level and is worth 50 per cent of the marks.

The full A-level qualification will normally be made up of six modules. The first three modules form the AS level for the subject. Vocational AS and A-levels have a similar structure. There is a three-unit vocational AS in Business, Engineering, Health & Social Care, and Information Technology. A six-unit vocational course is a full A-level. This standardisation of structure makes it much easier to mix and match Vocational AS and A-levels and other A/AS levels.

The subjects you have taken at GCSE are bound to influence your choice of A/AS levels. A/AS levels are of a high standard and in some subjects it may not be easy to cope with the A/AS level syllabus unless you have studied the subject on a GCSE course – Languages and Sciences are examples of this. So, ask yourself which A/AS levels you might want to do before choosing your GCSEs.

Some of the subjects offered at A/AS level include the learning of specific practical skills. In some schools and colleges you can study Dance, Art or Sports Studies at A/AS level.

Other options in the sixth form or at college

Many schools and colleges offer Foundation or Intermediate Level GNVQ courses for students in Year 12 onwards, although these will no longer be available after 2007.

For GNVQ Intermediate courses students have normally been expected to have achieved something like four GCSEs at grades D–G or a Foundation GNVQ (or an NVQ at Level 1).

Entry onto GNVQ Foundation Level courses does not require any formal qualifications, although applicants need to show the ability to benefit from the course.

You may find that you are also able to take GCSEs in the sixth form. These are usually two-year courses, but sometimes there is the option of one-year courses, especially in new subject areas. Coursework will still normally be a feature of these courses, but the syllabus will be designed to ensure you can carry it out within one year.

15. Making the choice

The National Curriculum has limited the number of options open to students in Years 10 and 11 (Years 11 and 12 in Northern Ireland). However, with greater flexibility being re-introduced into the KS4 curriculum, it is important that you should think carefully about your choice. This book should have helped you get all the facts you need. You should now be ready to make your final choice.

Use this checklist to make your selection.

- Make a list of all the subjects your school is offering.
- Tick subjects that are essential for your career.
- Tick all the subjects your school insists that you take.
- Tick any subjects you enjoy/are good at/want to take.
- Tick any of the new subjects being offered that you would like to try or think would be useful.
- Check to see if you have at least one subject from each of the major subject groups, i.e.:
  - English
  - Maths
  - Modern Foreign Languages
  - Sciences
  - Humanities
  - Creative Subjects (including Technology)

  and make sure you have taken advice before leaving out any one group.
- Count up the number of subjects you have ticked. If it comes to more than six, check with your teachers how many subjects they think you can cope with.

- Check the coursework commitment in each subject with your teachers.
- If there are too many subjects or the coursework commitment is too high, work through this list again, being more selective.
- Remember that there are other people as well as your subject teachers who you can talk to – your Connexions Personal Adviser or Careers Adviser, careers teacher, form tutor, year tutor and, of course, your family.

Now, how does it look?
Horrendous?
Horrifying?
Difficult?

Look through the checklist again and be even more selective.
Or:
Hard work?
Interesting?
OK?

Just right?
GO FOR IT!

But what if I do choose the wrong subjects – what can I do?

Don't panic! It happens all the time.

It could be that you will suddenly get a new career idea and will realise you need to be studying something else. If you have chosen wisely in the first place, it is unlikely that many of the subjects you have opted for will be wrong. So, if you are part way through your GCSEs, the answer is to keep on studying and get the best grades you can in the subjects you are taking. That will always stand you in good stead. Who knows, you might change your mind yet again.

Then, when you get to the sixth form or move on to a college, you can take the extra subjects you need. Because you will be that much older, you should be able to take them in one year instead of the normal two – that is one of the advantages of the GCSE system.

My GCSE decisions
Subject groups
English   Maths   Sciences
Humanities   Creative Subjects
Modern Languages

1. _____

2. _____

3. _____

Other sources of reference

Your school's *Options* booklet

Which Way Now? (Connexions). This information guide for Year 9 students gives lots of information and advice about your choices and their implications for later career decisions and routes. It is available free by phoning 0845 60 222 60 and is also available on the Internet – www.connexions-direct.com/whichwaynow.

Which Way Now? Study Decisions at 14 (Careers Scotland). You can get copies of this publication by phoning 0131 625 6555. It is also available on the Internet, via www.careers-scotland.org.uk.

Subjects and exams for 14- to 16-year-olds (QCA) (available also in Bengali, Chinese, Greek, Gujarati, Hindi, Punjabi, Turkish, Urdu, Vietnamese and in Braille and on cassette). Phone 020 8561 4499.

GCSE Regulations and Criteria (QCA/ACCAC).

GCSEs in vocational subjects (DfES – free) – *an introduction for students and their carers*). This leaflet is a general introduction to the qualifications.
    General information about education is available on the Parents Centre section of the DfES website, at www.dfes.gov.uk/parents.

An A–Z of Exam Survival (Trotman). www.trotman.co.uk.